SEASON OF ASH AND FIRE

Season of Ash and Fire

PRAYERS AND LITURGIES FOR
LENT AND EASTER

Blair Gilmer Meeks

ABINGDON PRESS
Nashville

SEASON OF ASH AND FIRE
PRAYERS AND LITURGIES FOR LENT AND EASTER

Copyright © 2003 by Abingdon Press

This book is printed on recycled, acid-free, elemental-chlorine–free paper.

Library of Congress Cataloging in Publication Data

Meeks, Blair Gilmer.
    Season of ash and fire : prayers and liturgies for Lent and Easter / Blair Gilmer Meeks.
      p. cm.
Includes index.
    ISBN 0-687-04454-5
    1. Lent—Prayer-books and devotions—English. 2. Liturgics. I. Title.

BV85.M44 2004
264—dc22

2003018971

Scripture quotations are from the New Revised Standard Version of the Bible, copyright © 1989, by the Division of Christian Education of the National Council of the Churches of Christ in the United States of America. Used by permission.

03 04 05 06 07 08 09 10 11 12 – 10 9 8 7 6 5 4 3 2 1

MANUFACTURED IN THE UNITED STATES OF AMERICA

To Doug

Celebrating our forty years
as partners in the dance

Contents

Introduction

Dancing at Easter

The sweep of the Easter cycle observances is breathtaking: from ashes to fire, from grief over our mortality and sin on Ash Wednesday to joy in the power of God's Holy Spirit given at Pentecost, the seal of God's new creation in Jesus Christ. Fourteen Sundays and the holy feasts among them. Nearly one hundred days. Almost a third of the year. The holiest season of the year.

The traditions of Lent and Easter are as old as they come for Christian worship. Part of our sense of renewal is discovering just how ancient they are and joining the faithful, myriads of myriads and thousands of thousands, whose mourning has been turned to dancing with each new celebration of Easter. If we speak publicly of our faith at all, we speak of the events that we acclaim in this season, and we rely on words that have come down to us from the prayers and songs of long ago.

The prayers in this book are written to reflect the tradition but do so in contemporary language and with an awareness of the situation and concerns of modern worshipers. They are based on the Scriptures that have for generations shaped our worship during Lent and Easter. I have relied for the most part on the readings from the Revised Common Lectionary, but the themes and emphases of the prayers are ones we hold in common and the biblical texts are often the ones also chosen by those who do not usually follow the lectionary. Because the Prayer for Illumination immediately precedes the sermon, I have included specific prayers for each of the lectionary cycles for that one element of the liturgy. This is intended to assist lectionary preachers and offer nonlectionary preachers alternative "lead-ins" to their sermons.

I have concentrated mainly on the Sundays in Lent and Easter. Fine worship resources for the special celebrations are available in all the recent denominational books of worship and are remarkable for their ecumenical convergence. *The New Handbook of the Christian Year* (Hoyt L. Hickman, Don E. Saliers, Laurence Hull Stookey, and James F. White, Nashville: Abingdon Press, 1992) is a full compendium of celebrations, written in conversation with the ecumenical liturgical dialogue. It also contains invaluable commentary for those preparing worship in all denominations.

For Ash Wednesday, Holy Thursday, Good Friday, the Easter Vigil, and Ascension Day, I have offered some suggestions for planning celebrations that follow the traditional pattern but allow smaller congregations and others whose resources are limited to plan in new, less daunting ways. I have also tried in the Sunday celebrations to be aware of the need for new ideas that do not require elaborate equipment or specialized staff. For the Sundays of Lent and Easter in this book, for example, the Acts of Praise are simple dramas or responsive readings, sometimes with congregational singing, that can be used in almost any church situation.

For each Sunday I have followed the order of worship used in many Presbyterian, Methodist, and United Church of Christ congregations. The prayers can, of course, be adapted to fit particular needs and also may be useful in other settings. The Acts of Praise, for example, may serve as the opening worship at a small group meeting; the youth fellowship or chancel drama group can perform a dramatic scene or reading for nursing center residents or at a church party.

Additional resources for use during the season also include prayers for household worship and opening prayers for study groups and church meetings, found in part Four, "Extending the Celebration." For those planning small group Bible study sessions during Lent, see the suggestions found on page 133.

This is an Easter book in the same way the whole season is called the Easter cycle, not the Lent/Easter cycle. The death and resurrection of Jesus Christ, which we celebrate as one event over the Great Three Days, is the focus of all our prayers. We cannot face the reality of our own death and sin on Ash Wednesday or call Jesus "King" on Palm Sunday if we do not know that God has raised Jesus from the dead and given to us the power of the resurrection in our lives now. "Easter" no longer refers in liturgical terminology to one day only. The day of resurrection is Easter Day, or more traditionally, the Paschal Feast. There is no possibility that the power of the resurrection can be celebrated adequately in one day or one lifetime. The season of Easter lasts fifty days, a Jubilee of days, with implications for the way we live together always in God's favor. The number fifty speaks of perfection, eternity. It carries with it the associations of the Jubilee year in Leviticus 25 when the earth was replenished, slaves were freed, lands reclaimed, debts canceled, and all God's people renewed: the year when God's justice and peace prevailed. That is what Easter begins again for us. We are made new by the death and resurrection of Jesus Christ, and we live in God's resurrection household, not just for a day or a lifetime but forever.

My thanks go especially to Laurence Stookey, who, by his work and friendship, has oriented me toward Easter. His book *Calendar: Christ's Time for the Church* (Nashville: Abingdon Press, 1996) is a vital resource for my work and for anyone who marks time by the liturgical seasons.

Every day I am thankful to Douglas Meeks. His theological reflection is located firmly in the resurrection household, and his Easter singing and dancing fill the home we have shared for forty years with joy and hope.

> The Christian faith begins with Easter singing and dancing, with Easter laughter, or it has not begun at all. We have to live and speak the gospel publicly. . . . How do we do that? Where is our singing and dancing? . . .
>
> That's the secret of our life of baptism, whether we see and hear the power that creates a new resurrection household. Will we go in? Are we ready to dance? But entering the household of Jesus Christ means that we will have to be changed, not of our own power but out of the grace and power given to us by the gospel.*

---

*M. Douglas Meeks, "Speaking the Gospel Publicly in North America," *Liturgy*, 9:2 (Winter 1990): 9-15.

PART ONE

The Sundays
in Lent

Introduction

At the name of Jesus every knee should bend,
in heaven and on earth and under the earth,
and every tongue should confess that Jesus Christ is Lord,
to the glory of God the Father. (Philippians 2:10-11)

Sundays are not counted in the total of the forty days of Lent. Even during Lent, Sunday is celebrated as a resurrection day and thus a day for praise and thanksgiving. Falling within the season of Lent, however, these Sundays do have a special focus and significance. The Sunday scripture readings during this season give us opportunity for serious reflection on our need to repent, that is, turn again toward God, and prepare for the coming crucifixion/resurrection observance. This reflection and self-examination is always guided by our trust in the resurrection of the Crucified One.

Beginning with Ash Wednesday we reflect on our fallibility and mortality, our need for forgiveness and the power of resurrection. But Lent is not centered on personal penitence and confrontation with the reality of death alone. Lent is especially significant for the formation of the community of faith that arises from Jesus' act of love in his death and resurrection. Through this act Jesus brings new life to us as individuals but also as Christ's body. Lenten worship is therefore a source of hope for our gathered reality as the church, as well as a time of earnest reflection for each of us.

Older members of the congregation may remember when churches engaged in mission study at this time of year, and the mission of the church is a Lenten theme not to be neglected. In particular, we are drawn to Jesus' call for justice: freedom for the oppressed, release of the captives, good news to the poor, recovery of sight to the blind (Luke 4:18). Taking up our cross includes taking on Jesus' mission and confronting the powers of death in all its forms: terror and tyranny, corruption and greed, disregard for creation, and all the forces that prevent God's people from living life in its fullest. Studying social issues affecting our society from the perspective of our faith and engaging in mission projects that confront social problems are integral parts of our Lenten discipline, remembering that God sent Jesus, not to save only a few good people, but to save the whole world. Our corporate prayers will reflect our concern for the world and our interconnectedness with all creation.

The earliest Lenten traditions we know about speak of a time of fasting and preparation that lasted only a few days before the solemn, night-long Paschal Vigil when early Christians remembered Christ as the Passover Lamb. But by the fourth century, Easter had become the principal celebration for baptisms, and the converts who were to be baptized needed more than a few days for instruction and preparation. The idea that there should be forty days probably comes from the many references to forty-day or forty-year periods in the Bible: Noah's forty days on the waters of the flood, and Moses', Elijah's, and Jesus' times in the wilderness.

We still associate Lent with preparation for participation in the communion of God and membership in Christ's body. Confirmation and new member classes often meet during Lent. Many congregations also have small group sessions for longtime, active members designed to deepen their understanding of Scripture and the church. A reaffirmation of baptismal vows is part of the Easter Vigil service found in newer denominational worship books. Thus, because we are preparing to take part at Easter in a renewal of the promises that were made for us when we were infants or that we made ourselves some time ago, the meaning of baptism is emphasized during Lent. According to the theology Paul articulates in Romans 6:1-12, baptism is our sacramental way of participating in Christ's death and resurrection: "For if we have been united with him in a death like his, we will certainly be united with him in a resurrection like his" (v. 5). Another baptismal text that figures strongly in our Lenten reflection is the hymn in Philippians 2:5-11, which encourages us to "Let the same mind be in you that was in Christ Jesus."

The resurgence of Lenten observance in recent years reflects an urgent need to introduce new members from a variety of backgrounds to Christian traditions and Scriptures and to deepen the appreciation of longtime members for the most significant of all the holy seasons. In our society it is especially crucial that we reflect on the way Jesus expects disciples to live. Lent offers an opportunity to practice that alternate lifestyle by spending more time in personal devotion, engaging more frequently in corporate worship, and working in mission projects; that is, it is a time for changing the way we do things. Lent, then, helps us show by our lives that we are not bound to the old ways but are willing to lose the old life and take up the new life Jesus offers. We observe the ancient Lenten disciplines of penitence, study, prayer, fasting, almsgiving; we keep our eyes on the cross where Christ was lifted up; and we grow as individuals and as a community of faith.

This section contains prayers for each of the Sundays in Lent that can be used or adapted for use in various settings. The prayers are based on themes suggested by the Revised Common Lectionary readings for each Sunday in Lent, but they are also appropriate for the season in congregations that do not follow the lectionary.

For each Sunday I have suggested a "theme symbol" and given a few sentences of comment on that theme. These comments are meant to serve as a guide for worship planners to the movement of the season as it progresses from Ash Wednesday to Palm Sunday and to help focus the parts of the worship service. All the themes occur and recur in the readings and prayers for all the Sundays during Lent, so no one theme should dominate in a particular worship service. Our need for repentance, God's gift of the covenant, living water that leads to eternal life, Jesus' lifting up on the cross of humiliation and glory: all are vital for our worship, and these themes are repeated and interact with each other throughout the season.

The symbols suggested below, which offer a concrete way to visualize the themes of the Lenten Scriptures, may be used in a variety of ways, but it is not appropriate to place these objects on the altar or communion table. No objects other than those used in the celebration of communion belong on the table. The theme symbols for each Sunday can be used, however, in ways that will not interfere with the central symbols of the worship space. One possibility is to place a small table near the door by which the congregation enters the sanctuary and arrange the suggested objects on this table, beginning on the first Sunday in Lent with the stones and adding an object each week. The objects may also be placed on tables that serve as worship centers in classrooms or homes, and they may be the subject of art on bulletin covers.

First Sunday in Lent

Theme Symbol: Wilderness

The wilderness can be represented by rocks. Place a few fist-sized rocks directly on a table or arrange them in a shallow pottery container of sand.

The Gospel reading for the first Sunday of Lent is traditionally an account of Jesus' encounter with the tempter; the epistle readings point us toward his ultimate act of self-giving. These scriptures direct our attention this Sunday to Jesus, who shares all our trials and leads us at last to victory in his cross and resurrection.

Call to Worship

> To you, O Lord, we lift up our souls.
>
> **Teach us your ways, O Lord;**
> **show us your paths and lead us in your truth.**
>
> Trust in God, who will not put you to shame;
> be glad in the Lord and rejoice in God's justice.
>
> **Shout for joy, all you upright in heart!**
> *(Based on Psalms 25 and 32)*

Opening Prayer

> God our help, you have given your angels charge over us
>   to guard us in all our ways:
> Make known your presence with us
>   throughout these forty days
> that we may find even in the wilderness
>   your springs of living water,

your touch that makes us whole.
In Jesus' name. **Amen.**

Call to Confession

Christ our Lord was tempted in the wilderness and knows all our trouble and weakness. We therefore have courage to confess our failings and our sins, knowing that the God of Jesus Christ will hear and forgive us.

Prayer of Confession

God of mercy,
we confess that we too often satisfy our own desires before we think of others;
we take needless risks that endanger ourselves and those around us;
we look for power in the wrong places and fail to let you rule in our lives.
Help us to turn away from all that keeps us from worshiping you alone.
In Jesus' name. Amen.

Words of Assurance

Jesus dismissed the tempter and walked from the wilderness toward the glory of the cross. Let us rejoice this day in Jesus' glorious victory through his death and resurrection. In Jesus' name we are forgiven.

Acts of Praise   *Thanksgiving for God's Gifts*
A Time of Prayer and Meditation

Six strong readers, perhaps from a chancel drama group, present the following meditation and prayer of thanksgiving for the beginning of Lent.

Leader:
God's people were rescued from slavery in Egypt and wandered for forty years. They learned in the wilderness to depend on God alone for their most basic needs: They ate manna and

drank water from the rock. As we begin our Lenten journey, let us give thanks and pray for God's gifts that bring us life. After each thanksgiving, we will keep a brief silence for reflection.

Voice One:
"[God] humbled you by letting you hunger, then by feeding you with manna, with which neither you nor your ancestors were acquainted, in order to make you understand that one does not live by bread alone, but by every word that comes from the mouth of the LORD." *(Deuteronomy 8:3)*

We give thanks, O God, for your Bread from Heaven.
Silence

Voice Two:
"If I take the wings of the morning and settle at the farthest limits of the sea, even there your hand shall lead me, and your right hand shall hold me fast." *(Psalm 139:9-10)*

We give thanks, O God, for your Presence with us.
Silence

Voice Three:
"For the mountains may depart and the hills be removed, but my steadfast love shall not depart from you, and my covenant of peace shall not be removed, says the LORD, who has compassion on you." *(Isaiah 54:10)*

We give thanks, O God, for your great Compassion.
Silence

Voice Four:
"The Lord does not deal with us according to our sins, nor repay us according to our iniquities. For as the heavens are high above the earth, so great is the Lord's steadfast love toward the faithful; as far as the east is from the west, so far does the Lord remove our transgressions from us."
(Psalm 103:10-12, The United Methodist Hymnal)

We give thanks, O God, for your Forgiveness.
Silence

Voice Five:
"Then the angel showed me the river of the water of life, bright as crystal, flowing from the throne of God and of the Lamb through the middle of the street of the city."

(Revelation 22:1-2a)

We give thanks, O God, for your grace that leads us to eternal Life through Jesus Christ.
Silence

Leader:
Let us pray.
God, our companion and guide, bless our journey of renewal and hope. Lead us together toward the celebration of Jesus' death and resurrection. Grant us grace to be a community of love, bringing your word of life to the world you sent your Son to save. In Jesus' name. Amen.

Hymn Suggestions: ***"I Want a Principle Within," "Lord, I Want to Be a Christian"***

Prayer for Illumination

Year A
God of life, your Son brings an end
to the dominance of death:
Fill us now with words of hope
that we may serve life in your name,
through Jesus Christ our Lord. **Amen.**

Year B
We appeal to you, God,
through the resurrection of Jesus Christ:
Create in us clean hearts
and renew in us the spirit of our baptism
that we may hear and do your word of life. **Amen.**

Year C
Remind us, O God,
that your word is near to us:

on our lips and in our heart.
Lead us by your Spirit
through the wilderness of doubt and fear
to call upon your name. **Amen.**

Prayer of Thanksgiving after the Offering

God of abundant grace, in thankfulness
we celebrate the bounty that you have given to us.
Grant us generous hearts that our gifts may do your work
and our lives may reflect your love, freely given to us
through the death and resurrection
of Jesus Christ our Savior. **Amen.**

Prayers of Intercession

Loving God, you sent your angels to wait on Jesus after his
time of trial;
send your comfort to those who wait in the wilderness for your
healing waters.

Have mercy on us, O God, in whom we trust.

Free us from the hosts of evil, the fear and doubt that bind us.

Have mercy on us, O God, in whom we trust.

Calm the raging nations as you still the roaring sea.

Have mercy on us, O God, in whom we trust.

Bring your healing balm to cure our souls, sick of sin and
bound to death.

Have mercy on us, O God, in whom we trust.

Lead us to follow our friend Jesus to the cross and to his victory
over death.

Have mercy on us, O God, in whom we trust.

Bring us to your salvation through the resurrection of Jesus
Christ, who is at the right hand of God,
with angels, authorities, and powers made subject to him.

Lord, have mercy.
Christ, have mercy.
Lord, have mercy. Amen.

Commission and Blessing

After Noah and his family lived forty days with the waters of
the flood, God made with him and with all the earth a covenant
of peace, signified by a bow in the sky. Let us now go in peace,
assured that God's love reigns over us.

The peace of Christ go with you.

And also with you.

Second Sunday in Lent

Theme Symbol: Water

Next to the rocks on the table, place a large, clear glass bowl of
water.

We are led by today's scriptures from remembering God's
covenant with the faithful, beginning with Abraham, to joining the
disciples as they learn about Jesus' coming suffering, death, and
resurrection, and to our response through the covenant we make at
our baptism.

Call to Worship

One thing I ask of the Lord
that will I seek after:

I will dwell in the Lord's house
all the days of my life,
to behold the beauty of the Lord
and inquire in the Lord's temple.

Wait for the Lord,
be strong and let your heart take courage,

Wait for the Lord!

(Based on Psalms 22 and 27)

Opening Prayer

God of the covenant,
through your promise of life to Abraham and Sarah,
you bless countless generations and touch all creation:
Turn us again toward your abundant life,
made ours through Jesus Christ.
Prepare us in this holy season
to reaffirm with all your church our covenant of baptism.
In the name of Jesus, who reigns with you and the Holy Spirit;
Amen.

Call to Confession

Because we are citizens of God's righteous reign, Jesus calls on us
to repent, that is, to turn toward God, take up our cross, and
leave behind all that keeps us from following Jesus. Let us
acknowledge before God and this congregation our need for
repentance.

Prayer of Confession

God of glory,
you sent your Son Jesus to die that we might have life:
Show us the ways we fail to answer your call.
Keep us from being bound to possessions,
from longing for outward approval,
from listening to voices that distract us from your word,
from hesitating to lose our old lives and take up your new life.
Our help comes from you, O Lord; keep us from all evil.
In Jesus' name. Amen.

Words of Assurance

Jesus our Lord was handed over to death for our trespasses. The God who raised this same Jesus from the dead welcomes those who truly repent in Jesus' name and will transform us to conform to his glory. Thanks be to God.

Acts of Praise   **"Lift Up Your Eyes"**—*A Responsive Reading*
Based on verses from Genesis 15; Psalms 22, 27, 121; John 3; Mark 8; Romans 4; Philippians 3

Leader: God told Abraham to lift up his eyes and see the stars as a sign of God's promise. Abraham believed and his faith was counted as righteousness.

People: **We lift up our eyes to the hills. Our help comes from the Lord.**

L: Like Abraham we stand firm in our faith. Our faith is in God who raised Jesus from the dead.

P: **I believe that I shall see the goodness of the Lord in the land of the living.**

L: Jesus told his disciples that he would suffer greatly, be rejected and killed, and on the third day rise again.

P: **We proclaim God's deliverance to future generations, saying "The Lord has done it!"**

L: Jesus said to Nicodemus, "No one can see God's reign without being born from above. No one can enter God's reign without being born of water and the Spirit."

P: **The Lord is my light and my salvation; whom shall I fear?**

L: Jesus invited Nicodemus to lift up his eyes to the cross, to see the Savior who descended to live among us, now ascended and exalted.

P: **God sent the Son into the world, not to condemn the world, but that the world might be saved through him.**

L: We too are invited to see Jesus, lifted up on the cross of suffering for the world, and lifted on high to reign in glory with God and the Holy Spirit, one God now and forever.

P: **All the ends of the earth shall remember and turn to the Lord, for dominion belongs to the Lord who rules over the nations. Lift up your eyes.**

Hymn Suggestion: ***"Lift High the Cross"***

Prayer for Illumination

Year A
Creator God, you give life to the dead
and call all things into existence:
Teach us to hear your promises
and testify to what we know,
for we are born of the Spirit
and look to Jesus for eternal life.
In his name we pray. **Amen.**

Year B
God of glory,
you are able to do what you promise:
Grant us grace to grow strong in our faith
that we may take up Jesus' cross
and receive his gift of life,
through his death and resurrection. **Amen.**

Year C
Gather us, O God, as a hen gathers her chicks.
Give us willing hearts, ready to receive your word
so that we may stand firm,
expecting our Savior Jesus Christ,
who has power to rule over all.
In his name. **Amen.**

Prayer of Thanksgiving After the Offering

Generous God, you do not ask us for tokens or tributes:
You ask that the poor shall eat and be satisfied,
that those who seek you shall praise your name.
Receive the gifts we bring with our thanksgiving
and hear our songs of grateful praise.
In Jesus' name. **Amen.**

Prayers of Intercession and Thanksgiving

Good and merciful God, we give you thanks that through our baptism we have died to sin and been raised to walk with Christ in newness of life. We thank you for evidence of new life around us. Especially we thank you for

the faithful witness of your people.
God, in your goodness,

we give you thanks.

the love of friends and families.
God, in your goodness,

we give you thanks.

the energy to study, work, and play.
God, in your goodness,

we give you thanks.

the joy of children who are loved.
God, in your goodness,

we give you thanks.

Compassionate God, your love extends to the whole world: Open our eyes to the suffering of your people everywhere and give us the courage to make their needs our own. Especially we pray for

children who are neglected, abused, or oppressed.
Lord, in your mercy,

hear our prayer.

the sick and those who mourn.
Lord, in your mercy,

hear our prayer.

persons who are lonely and fearful
Lord, in your mercy,

hear our prayer.

those whose countries are torn by war.
Lord, in your mercy,

hear our prayer.

the hungry and the homeless.
Lord, in your mercy,

hear our prayer.

those who wait for justice and freedom.
Lord, in your mercy,

hear our prayer.

Walk with us every day
and send us to do your work in joy and thanksgiving
for all that you have done through Jesus Christ our Savior.
Amen.

Commission and Blessing

May we live in the promises of our baptism, for we are marked
with the sign of God the Father, God the Son, and God the
Holy Spirit, and we hold our citizenship in Christ's glorious
realm.

Thanks be to God.

The Lord's name be praised.

Third Sunday in Lent

Theme Symbol: The Cross

This week add a handmade, wooden cross or a cross purchased
from a third-world crafts store to the table of symbols.

As we move further into the season of Lent, we are drawn to the message of the cross: the life-giving power of Jesus' death and resurrection, a message that is misunderstood by many but becomes the water of life to the thirsty in a parched land.

Call to Worship

O come, let us sing to the Lord;
let us make a joyful noise to the rock of our salvation!

**Let us come into God's presence with thanksgiving;
let us make a joyful noise with songs of praise!**

Your steadfast love is better than life,
and our lips will praise you,
In the shadow of your wings we sing for joy.

**We will bless you as long as we live;
we will lift up our hands and call on your name.**

(Based on Psalms 63 and 95)

Opening Prayer

God of wisdom, your word revives our soul;
you give us a spring of water gushing up to eternal life:
Grant us grace to see and follow Jesus,
to offer his compassion to those in need,
to walk in the steps of his zeal for justice,
that we may worship you in spirit and truth.
In Jesus' name. **Amen.**

Call to Confession

Jesus was quick to denounce those who made the temple a marketplace, but he is slow to anger when we turn to him for help and forgiveness. Because we have access to God's grace, let us seek the peace of God through prayer and repentance.

Prayer of Confession

**God of grace, you call on us to repent, to endure, and to hope:
Strengthen us that we may work always for the common good.
We confess that though we look for sin in others,**

we are reluctant to examine ourselves;
we are caught up in worldly wisdom and forget your words;
we complain about troubles and fail to see your good gifts.
Have patience with us and nurture us that we may grow in
love,
for the sake of your Son Jesus Christ. Amen.

Words of Assurance

While we were still sinners Christ died for us. We have been jus-
tified by his blood, and we are saved by his life. This is proof
of God's love for us. Thanks be to God for God will abundantly pardon.

Acts of Praise   **The Commandments**
A Choral Reading *Based on Matthew 22:36-40, Psalm
19, and John 15:12-14*
For one lead voice and a choir of readers

Lead Voice: Jesus was asked a question to test him:
"Teacher, which commandment in the law is the greatest?"

Choir of Readers: **The law of the Lord is perfect, reviving the
soul; the decrees of the Lord are sure, making wise the simple.**

LV: Jesus answered, "You shall love the Lord your God with all
your heart, and with all your soul, and with all your mind. This
is the greatest and first commandment."

CR: **The precepts of the Lord are right, rejoicing the heart:
the commandment of the Lord is clear, enlightening the eyes.**

LV: Then he said, "And a second is like it: 'You shall love your
neighbor as yourself.' On these two commandments hang all
the law and the prophets."

CR: **The fear of the Lord is pure, enduring forever;
the ordinances of the Lord are true and righteous altogether.**

LV: Later Jesus said to his disciples, "This is my commandment,
that you love one another as I have loved you. No one has
greater love than this, to lay down one's life for one's friends.
You are my friends if you do what I command you."

CR: **Let the words of our mouths and the meditation of our hearts be acceptable to you, O Lord, our rock and our redeemer.**

Hymn Suggestions: ***"Jesu, Jesu, Fill Us with Your Love,"***
"Jesus, United by Thy Grace"

Prayer for Illumination

Year A
God, through Christ you give us the water of life:
Make us thirsty for your word
that we may give witness to your great love,
poured into our hearts through the Holy Spirit.
In the name of Jesus Christ. **Amen.**

Year B
Faithful God, you save those who believe:
Enlighten us with your wisdom;
teach us to look beyond our foolish ways
and receive the message of the cross.
In the name of Jesus who died and was raised. **Amen.**

Year C
Compassionate God,
you give us tender care and time to grow:
Turn us toward you as to the sun's light.
Lead us to drink from the spiritual rock that is Christ,
receiving from you the life he came to give. **Amen.**

Prayer of Thanksgiving After the Offering

Gracious God, we are surrounded by your gifts:
Open our eyes and give us grateful hearts.
Teach us to give generously of all that we have
and to love each other according to your command.
Help us to remember with thanksgiving our salvation
through the death and resurrection of Jesus Christ our Lord,
in whose name we pray. **Amen.**

Prayers of Intercession and Thanksgiving

God, our Savior and Deliverer,
you gave our ancestors water from the rock
and shielded them from harm in the desert:
Protect us now from fear and doubt;
give us the water that leads to eternal life.
Bring us into your peace through our Lord Jesus Christ.

Pour your Spirit into your church
that it may remain faithful to your word
and be united in love.
God of grace,

Hear our prayer.

Guide the leaders of the nations
that they may love justice
and work for the good of all.
God of grace,

Hear our prayer.

Teach us the way of peace
that we may live in love and reconciliation
with all peoples.
God of grace,

Hear our prayer.

Comfort the lonely and those who sorrow;
heal the sick and those in despair.
Give us compassion for the needy
and those who suffer injustice.
God of grace,

Hear our prayer.

Receive our thanks for your goodness to us:
for the gifts of water and word;
for the communion of your church;
for the love of friends and family;
for the gladness of your tender care.

Keep us safe beneath your wings
and bring us to the joy of Jesus' resurrection,
through which we all are saved.
In his name we pray. **Amen.**

Commission and Blessing

The Samaritan woman gave Jesus water to drink, listened to his words about the water of life, and went to tell the people that a man from God was in their midst. As we leave this place, let us become witnesses to Jesus' death and resurrection.

Praise be to God whose glory rises from the heavens and circles
   the earth.
The Holy One of Israel freely offers a feast of rich food and
   wine.
Jesus our Savior pours us water from the spring of eternal life.
The Spirit of truth reconciles us to God and gives us peace.

Thanks be to God. Amen.

Fourth Sunday in Lent

Theme Symbol: Light
Use a single, white pillar candle.

A part of our Lenten discipline is to look at the effect of sin in our lives. The writers of the psalms saw that unconfessed sin can make us ill. Jesus calls for repentance and points to the dire consequences of sin and evil, but he refuses to link specific instances of suffering or disability directly to an individual's sin. This Sunday's readings point us to the gift of seeing: the way Jesus sees us and the way we see Jesus, who offers healing and forgiveness through the power of the resurrection.

Call to Worship

O give thanks to the Lord, who is good;
whose steadfast love endures forever.

**Let us give thanks for the steadfast love of the Lord,
for God's wonderful works to humankind.**

Let the redeemed of the Lord tell their story,
those whom God redeemed from trouble.

**Be glad in the Lord and rejoice, O righteous,
Shout for joy, all you upright in heart.**

(Based on Psalms 32 and 107)

Opening Prayer

God of light, you do not see as others see;
you look beyond our limitations
and find us strong and beautiful for your purpose.
Help us now to see Jesus your Son
who, though he was despised and rejected,
became our beautiful Savior.
Show us Jesus' face in the face of those who suffer
and lead us to give your healing touch to all.
In Jesus' name. **Amen.**

Call to Confession

When we keep silent about our sins, we are burdened and
weak. But if we acknowledge our sins before God, God will
forgive and heal us. Let all who are faithful offer prayer in
times of distress. Let us confess our transgressions to the Lord.

Prayer of Confession

**God our Redeemer, you welcome us
with the unbounded love of a parent for a lost child:
Help us when we turn away from your safekeeping;
watch over us when we choose the far country of doubt
and fear;**

guide us back with thoughts of the place you have prepared
   for us;
forgive us when we fail to see Jesus, sent from you.
Turn our eyes toward the cross where he was lifted up for us.
In his name we pray. Amen.

Words of Assurance

"Happy are those who are forgiven, who stand among the righteous surrounded by the steadfast love of the Lord." By the
power of Jesus' death and resurrection, we are forgiven and
healed.   *(Author's paraphrase, based on Psalm 32:1, 10)*

Acts of Praise   **Thanksgiving for the Light**
                     Dramatic Reading for Three Voices

*(Voice 1 stands at the pulpit, Voice 2 at the lectern, and
Voice 3 in the center. The readers should have strong
but varied voices, and the pace of their reading should
be upbeat, neither too slow nor too fast. Voice 3, however, should generally read more slowly than the others.)*

Voice 1: Give thanks to God, by whom we share in the saints'
inheritance of the light. *(Based on Colossians 1:12)*

Voice 2: "By the tender mercy of our God,
the dawn from on high will break upon us,
to give light to those who sit in darkness and in the shadow of
   death,
to guide our feet into the way of peace." *(Luke 1:78-79)*

Voice 3: Again Jesus spoke to them, saying, "I am the light of
the world. Whoever follows me will never walk in darkness
but will have the light of life." *(John 8:12)*

Voice 1: "You are the light of the world. . . . No one after lighting a lamp puts it under the bushel basket, but on the lamp-
stand, and it gives light to all in the house. In the same way, let
your light shine before others, so that they may see your good
works and give glory to your Father in heaven."

(Matthew 5:14-16)

Voice 2: "We must work the works of the One who sent me while it is day; night is coming when no one can work. As long as I am in the world, I am the light of the world."

(Based on John 9:4-5)

Voice 3: It was now about noon, and darkness came over the whole land until three in the afternoon, while the sun's light failed; and the curtain of the temple was torn in two.

(Luke 23:44-45)

Voice 1: In him was life, and the life was the light of all people.

(John 1:4)

Voice 2: The apostle Paul, with help from God, testified to King Agrippa, before small and great alike, saying nothing but what the prophets and Moses said would take place: that the Messiah must suffer, and by being the first to rise from the dead, would proclaim light both to his people and to the Gentiles. *(Acts 26:22-23, paraphrased)*

Voice 3: While you have the light, believe in the light, so that you may become children of light. *(John 12:36)*

Voice 1: If we walk in the light as God is in the light, we have fellowship with one another, and the blood of Jesus, God's Son, cleanses us from all sin. *(1 John 1:7, paraphrased)*

Voice 2: Children of God, you will shine like stars in the world.

(Philippians 2:15, paraphrased)

Voice 3: The city has no need of sun or moon to shine on it, for the glory of God is its light, and its lamp is the Lamb. The nations will walk by its light, and the kings of the earth will bring their glory into it. *(Revelation 21:23-24)*

Voice 1: For once you lived in shadow, but now in the Lord you are light. Live as children of light, enjoying all that is good and right and true. Try to find out what is pleasing to the Lord. "Sleeper, awake! Rise from the dead, and Christ will shine on you." *(Ephesians 5:8-14, paraphrased)*

Hymn Suggestions: **"I Want to Walk as a Child of the Light,"**
"Christ, Whose Glory Fills the Skies"

Prayer for Illumination

> *Year A*
> God our healer, you chose David,
> though he was young and only a shepherd:
> Wake us up to the light Christ shines on us.
> Show us what is good and right and true;
> open our eyes to the power of your resurrection.
> In Jesus' name. **Amen.**

> *Year B*
> God of our salvation,
> when we were kept down by sin,
> you raised us up with Christ:
> Show us the immeasurable riches of your grace
> that we may show the world
> the healing power of the cross.
> In the name of Jesus who died and was raised. **Amen.**

> *Year C*
> God, you trust us to be your messengers:
> Grant us courage to speak and act on your behalf.
> Give us your light
> that we may see beyond our fear
> and be at home with you.
> Through Christ our peace. **Amen.**

Prayer of Thanksgiving After the Offering

> God of grace, your glory is revealed
>   in the abundant gifts of your Son,
>   who is himself a gift beyond price:
> Make us generous with our neighbors,
>   multiply our gifts beyond our reach,
> and give us grace to join your joyful feast,
>   for you rule over all.
> In Jesus' name. **Amen.**

Prayers of Intercession

In peace let us pray to the Lord.

God, our Savior, you find us when we are lost;
you restore our sight so that we may see your glory:
Hear our prayers and keep us by your grace.

For the peace that is from above,
and the lovingkindness of God;

Let us pray to the Lord.

For the peace of the whole world and the unity of the church;

Let us pray to the Lord.

For those who help the poor, the strangers, and all sufferers,

Let us pray to the Lord.

For the sick and those who mourn,
for those who have requested us to remember them in prayer;
(here names may be read)

Let us pray to the Lord.

For those who struggle with doubt and fear,
and for those in despair;

Let us pray to the Lord.

For those who travel and those who are far from home;

Let us pray to the Lord.

For workers and students, for parents and teachers,
and for all who labor for you;

Let us pray to the Lord.

For the hearing of our prayer before God
and the sending down on us of God's tender mercies;

Let us pray to the Lord.

God, in your mercy, give us grace to live together in harmony with all people and by our lives to honor your name in thanksgiving for the gift of your Son Jesus Christ, who reigns with you and the Holy Spirit, one God, now and forever. Amen.

Commission and Blessing

Look and see how God has made all things new, for in Christ we are a new creation. All this is from God, who reconciled us through Christ, and gave us the ministry of peace. Let us go now as Christ's ambassadors, bringing to the world God's love and light.

Peace be with you.

And also with you.

Fifth Sunday in Lent

Theme Symbol: Stalks of Wheat

Dried wheat stalks are usually available from local farmers or florists, but if not, use an arrangement of a few tall stalks of dried grass with some seeds beside them.

This week's scripture readings point us to Jesus' death and the resurrection that is to come. The Gospels for the three-year lectionary cycle include Jesus' statement that he is "the resurrection and the life," the image of the grain of wheat that falls to the earth and dies so that it may bear fruit, and Mary of Bethany's anointing Jesus' feet in anticipation of his burial. We are waiting for the full joy of Easter, but we already have the hope and promise of new life.

Call to Worship

My soul waits for the Lord
more than those who watch for the morning,
more than those who watch for the morning.

**Hope in the LORD! For with the Lord there is steadfast love,
and great power to redeem.**

The LORD has done great things for us, and we rejoiced.
May those who sow in tears reap with shouts of joy.

**Those who go out weeping, bearing the seed for sowing,
shall come home with shouts of joy, carrying their sheaves.**

(Based on Psalms 130 and 126)

Opening Prayer

Mighty God, you make a way for us in the chaos of the sea
and give us water in desert places:
Help us to live by the covenant you write on our hearts;
open us to receive the new thing you are doing.
Give us grace to know Christ, the sharing of his sufferings,
and the power of his resurrection,
that we may gain the heavenly call of God in Christ Jesus. **Amen.**

Call to Confession

God has promised to restore us to joy and wholeness if we
acknowledge our sins and seek forgiveness. Therefore, remembering that there is forgiveness with God whom we revere, let
us ask God to take us by the hand and lead us to the throne of
grace.

Prayer of Confession

**Have mercy on us, O God, according to your steadfast love,
for we know our sins, and we cannot overlook them.
We have failed to put our complete confidence in you;
we rely on prestige and past success for reputation;
we look to the wealth and power of nations for support;
we cling to things, and yet knowing you surpasses all else.
Wash us; heal us; teach us to honor you with truth.
Let us know the joy and gladness of your saving grace
that we may have life through Jesus Christ our Lord. Amen.**

Words of Assurance

God has promised to forgive our iniquity and remember our sin no more. Let us set our minds on the Spirit and give praise to the One who raised Jesus from the dead.

Acts of Praise   **The Promise of Resurrection**
                    Based on Isaiah 43:18; Ezekiel 37:14; John 12:24, 32;
                    John 11:25, 40
                    A Responsive Reading

Leader: "Do not remember the former things, or consider the things of old. I am about to do a new thing; now it springs forth. Can you sense it? I will make a way in the wilderness and rivers in the desert."

People: **Jesus says if we believe, we will see the glory of God.**

L: "I will put my spirit within you, and you shall live, and I will place you on your own soil; then you shall know that I, the LORD, have spoken and will act."

P: **Jesus says if we believe, we will see the glory of God.**

L: "Unless a grain of wheat falls into the earth and dies, it remains just a single grain; but if it dies, it bears much fruit."

P: **Jesus says if we believe, we will see the glory of God.**

L: "And I, when I am lifted up from the earth, will draw all people to myself."
P: **Jesus says if we believe, we will see the glory of God.**

L: "I am the resurrection and the life. Those who believe in me, even though they die, will live."

P: **Yes, Lord, we believe that you are the Son of God, the one coming into the world, the resurrection and the life.**

Hymn Suggestions: *"Hope of the World," "Ask Ye What Great Thing I Know"*

Prayer for Illumination

> *Year A*
> Put your Spirit in us, O Lord;
> place us on home soil;
> make us alive to your word
> that we may believe.
> In the name of Jesus,
> the resurrection and the life. **Amen.**

> *Year B*
> God, you take us by the hand
> and write your word on our hearts:
> Teach us obedience
> that we may see Jesus,
> who heals all people by his perfect love.
> In the name of the One who was lifted up. **Amen.**

> *Year C*
> God our Deliverer,
> you invite us to see the new thing you are doing:
> Help us to know Christ and the power of his resurrection;
> lead us to respond with generous acts of love.
> In the name of Jesus. **Amen.**

Prayer of Thanksgiving After the Offering

> God of Life,
> we thank you for sending Jesus to glorify your name.
> You ask us always to be with the poor:
> Teach us to remember their needs
> and give our gifts without counting the cost,
> as we would give to your Son Jesus Christ,
> who reigns with you and the Holy Spirit. **Amen.**

Prayers of Intercession and Thanksgiving

> Holy God, you came to us in Jesus' life, death, and resurrection;
> we lift our hearts to you in thanksgiving for your wondrous
>   acts,
> and, mindful of your steadfast love,

we also lift before you the troubles of the world.

Merciful God, guide our thoughts to those in need;
guide our steps toward life and health and peace.

Restore us, O God. Our hope is in you.

Show us how to live
so that the earth's riches may benefit all earth's people.

Restore us, O God. Our hope is in you.

Teach us to care for your creation:
the deserts and the seas that you fill with your goodness,
the wild animals that honor you.

Restore us, O God. Our hope is in you.

Give us compassion to weep with those who mourn
and bring your healing to the sick.

Restore us, O God. Our hope is in you.

Give us courage to love each other in the name of Jesus
who draws all people to himself
by the power of his cross and resurrection.

Restore us, O God. Our hope is in you.

Help us to be your faithful people,
ready to be formed into one body,
ready to declare your praise.

Restore us, O God. Our hope is in you.

We give you thanks for the witness of those who came to see
    Jesus,
and for Jesus' presence with us now in word and sacrament.

The Lord has done great things. Thanks be to God.

We remember with thanksgiving our baptism
and the joy of being called your beloved children.

The Lord has done great things. Thanks be to God.

We rejoice in your promise of water in dry places,

new paths for those lost in despair,
new hope for those who live in death's shadow,
new life for all in the power of the resurrection.
The Lord has done great things. Thanks be to God. Amen.

Commission and Blessing

We are called to declare that Jesus Christ is the resurrection and the life. The God who leads us by the hand out of slavery to sin and death, the same God who writes a new covenant on our hearts, sends us the Spirit of life and peace to dwell in us.

Bless the Lord.

The Lord's name be praised. Amen.

Sixth Sunday in Lent: Palm/ Passion Sunday

Planning the Celebration

Palm/Passion Sunday is the bridge that connects Lent to our commemoration of Christ's crucifixion and resurrection. Its celebration prepares us for the events of the week that follows. The theme is Jesus' glory in his lowliness, his servanthood and kingship, and this paradox permeates the acclamation of the crowds in the palm procession and colors our understanding of the passion narrative reading. The worshipers should come prepared to hear both Gospel readings with the understanding that Jesus' choice of a lowly work animal to ride is the sign of his reign of peace, and Jesus' lifting up on the cross encompasses both his greatest humiliation and his exaltation.

In many traditions the Palm Gospel is read at the beginning of the service and the Passion Gospel at the end. One option for the preacher, who must preach between these two highly charged readings, is to choose as a text the often neglected epistle reading for the day, Philippians 2:5-11, which holds together the humility and glory of Christ, and illuminates his acceptance of death on the cross. This hymn and creed was probably used in early baptisms: we are admonished to "Let the same mind be in you that was in Christ Jesus," who willingly became a servant, subject to our every weakness, even death, and was therefore highly exalted by God.

Preparation for the service should be aimed at inviting worshipers to be Jesus' followers, ready to acclaim him even if in the face of doubt and fear at his arrest and execution. John's Gospel tells us that the crowd of followers who walked boldly with Jesus into Jerusalem was led by believers who witnessed Jesus' raising Lazarus from the dead (John 12:17). They "continued to testify" (v. 18) and therefore are unlikely to be part of the mob the Synoptic Gospels report at the trial who cried, "Crucify him." Many of those who proclaimed him Lord on Sunday ran and hid on Friday, but not all. A few stood before the cross with Jesus, and others, though their courage failed them, were among the large number of believers who had followed Jesus throughout his ministry and were opposed to those who wished to kill him. There is, in other words, a variety of possible responses to Jesus' arrest and execution: remaining faithful, turning away in fear, denial, rejection, and betrayal. We can ask ourselves what our response to Jesus is and we can join the mourners at Jesus' death. Even with our knowledge of his ultimate victory, we can weep in astonishment at the magnitude of God's self-giving love.

The palm procession represents an authentic outpouring of love and hope that the Promised One of God has come. For Jesus' followers who did not understand the foretelling of his death and resurrection, those expectations were dashed by the trial and execution, but they remembered this day and finally understood the events in light of his "glorification" (John 12:16).

Today's worshipers do know the outcome of Jesus' victory, and the "Hosannas" are for us shouts of assurance that Jesus is our salvation. There are shades of meaning, however, that color our celebration. First, this parade to Jerusalem was understood by the authorities to be a political act, a declaration that Jesus is God's Son and succeeds to David's throne in defiance of Rome's claim to lordship over the conquered people. Such an act elicited angry challenges from the authorities and momentous consequences. Jesus knew he was riding toward his own death. The Hosannas also reflect for us the original meaning of the acclamation—"Save us!"—for we live in a world where the fullness of Jesus' triumph over death is not yet realized, all tears have not yet been wiped away, and we are constantly aware of our need for salvation.

With all this in mind a children's parade around the sanctuary seems quite pale. In most celebrations, therefore, the whole congregation takes part and is encouraged to make themselves heard as well as seen entering the church. Jesus' entry into Jerusalem was, after all, accompanied by a noisy crowd; we are told that the stones would have shouted out if the people had kept silent. Singing is important in the procession but also other noise-making such as playing tambourines and clapping. Those who must remain seated may be given rhythm instruments to accompany the marchers or asked to clap in time to the music.

We have a written record of a palm procession that took place in Jerusalem in the late fourth century; it was a day-long march into the city by a community of young and old alike. The fact that Jesus was going into the city is sometimes used as a witness today by urban churches who hold their processions outdoors, often ecumenically with other congregations, and walk through the neighborhoods carrying the cross, adding people to the procession as they go along. Deciding how a congregation can make the procession both more participatory and more evocative of the events that follow is in itself a worthwhile endeavor. In all cases, the palm procession for today's congregations is an act of worship that invites us to participate now in the proclamation of Jesus' reign.

Theme Symbol: Branches and Palms

Palms have a strong association with this day, but using native branches for the procession—pussy willow, forsythia, pine, or marsh reeds—makes the point that we are praising Jesus now, not simply reenacting a past event.

Call to Worship

This is the day that the LORD has made;

let us rejoice and be glad in it.

This is the gate of the LORD;

the just shall enter through it.

This is the Lord's doing;

it is marvelous in our eyes.

Save us, we beg you, O LORD.

Blessed is the one who comes in the name of the LORD.

The LORD is God, and God has given us light.

Praise God on the way to the altar with branches.

O give thanks to the LORD, for God is good.

God's steadfast love endures forever.

(Based on Psalm 118:19-29)

Opening Prayer

God our strength,
you waken us morning by morning with your gracious word:
Help us to stand together against the enemies of life
and offer your mercy to the weary,
in the name of Jesus who did not hide his face
but stood firm before death to save the world. **Amen.**

Call to Confession

The Lord has need of us. The Lord asks us to come to the mercy seat, bringing our wounded hearts and our anguish, to lay our burdens before God that we may arise in wholeness and joy to follow Christ. Let us confess our sins.

Prayer of Confession

**Save us, O God, for we are surrounded by danger
and we live in death's shadow.
Forgive us when we fail to stand with the suffering,
when fear causes us to close our eyes to wrongdoing,
when weakness makes us turn back from following you.**

**Lift us up to the hope and healing of the cross;
make us bearers of the love of Jesus, poured out for the world.
In his name. Amen.**

Words of Assurance

It is the Lord God who helps us; who will declare us guilty? Giving thanks that God has answered us and become our salvation, let us greet each other with signs of peace.

(All are encouraged to greet each other with handshakes and embraces of peace, followed by the singing of a stanza of a familiar hymn, such as "Beautiful Savior" or "Amazing Grace.")

Acts of Praise   **At the Name of Jesus, Every Knee Shall Bow**
Philippians 2:5-11, read alternately by two groups in the congregation
(Suggestion: Women read light print; men read bold.)
(Based on The United Methodist Hymnal, #167)

Let the same mind be in you that was in Christ Jesus,
 who, though he was in the form of God, did not count equality with God a thing to be grasped,
but emptied himself,
 taking the form of a servant,
 being born in our likeness.
And being found in human form,
 he humbled himself and became obedient unto death
 even death on a cross.
Therefore God has highly exalted him
 and bestowed on him the name which is above every name,
that at the name of Jesus every knee shall bow,
 in heaven and on earth and under the earth,
and every tongue confess that Jesus Christ is Lord,
 to the glory of God the Father.

Hymn Suggestions: *"At the Name of Jesus," "All Hail the Power of Jesus' Name," "All Praise to Thee, for Thou O King Divine"*

49

Prayer for Illumination

> Holy God, waken our ears to your voice;
> teach us to listen and not turn backwards.
> Speak to us through your love on the cross
> that we may know your mercy, freely given,
> and show to all the world the glory of Jesus' name. **Amen.**

Prayer of Thanksgiving after the Offering

> Merciful God, your gift of love, immense and free, finds us out,
> makes a claim on our lives that we cannot ignore:
> Teach us to respond in thanksgiving,
> seeking, as did your Son, the poor and the outcast,
> giving of all that we have,
> in the name of Jesus Christ, Lord of heaven and earth. **Amen.**

Prayers of Intercession and Thanksgiving

> God, our salvation,
> your Son Jesus left your throne
> and emptied himself of all but love:
> Hear our prayer that we may have courage to go with Jesus
> and stand with him before all who oppose your word.
>
> Grant us healing that wars may cease,
> that violence and hate may be driven from the earth.
> Lord, hear our prayer.
>
> **Hosanna! Praise God for Jesus' reign of peace.**
>
> Grant us wisdom to choose just leaders
> and follow those who love your goodness.
> Lord, hear our prayer.
>
> **Hosanna! Praise God for Jesus' reign of peace.**
> Grant us compassion to visit the lonely,
> comfort the sick and sorrowing,
> and help those who wait for justice.
> Lord, hear our prayer.
>
> **Hosanna! Praise God for Jesus' reign of peace.**
>
> Grant us grace to live now in your community of love

where children are cared for, old people are valued,
and no one is left out.
Lord, hear our prayer.

Hosanna! Praise God for Jesus' reign of peace.

Lift our eyes to the crucified One;
lift our hearts to the exalted One, Jesus Christ,
who knows our fears and sorrows
and will lift us all to you.
We join your people everywhere in his song of praise:

"Blessed is the One who comes in the name of the Lord." Amen.

The Reading of the Passion Narrative

The passion narrative from one of the Synoptic Gospels—Matthew in Year A, Mark in Year B, and Luke in Year C—is often read at the very end of the Palm/Passion Sunday liturgy. The Revised Common Lectionary offers a long and a shorter version of each reading. Which one to use and how it will be read depends in part on how the reading of John's passion narrative on Good Friday is to be done. It is not advisable on either day to make the reading into a passion play with elaborate costumes and settings, but a dramatic reading along the lines of readers' theater may help make the familiar story more accessible to listeners. Those preparing to read will take the same care, deliberation, and reverence that is fitting for all Scripture reading in public worship. The text may be divided among three or more readers and does not need to be read so slowly that it drags. Since this is not a history pageant but a liturgical act, avoid predictable choices for the readers who will do specific parts. A member of the clergy should not always read Jesus' words, for example, and the congregation should not always take the part of the crowd. If the reading is to be well received and is seen as part of the people's preparation for the coming celebration of Easter, the readers will rehearse effectively and work to understand the consequences of the story they are presenting. The passion narratives from Matthew, Mark, and Luke in dramatic reading format are found on pages 135-52 of The New Handbook of the Christian Year *(Hoyt L. Hickman, et al., Nashville: Abingdon Press, 1992).*

Commission and Blessing

The worship leaders and readers may leave the church in silence at the end of the reading. No commission or blessing is given, the choir does not process, and no dismissal music is played. Worshipers may remain in silence as long as they wish. If, however, the passion Gospel is read before the sermon, a hymn and a blessing such as the following will come at the end of the service.

Years A and B

Let this mind be in us that was in Christ Jesus,
who became a servant that we might be free,
humbling himself to death on the cross
for the salvation of the world.

"Truly this man is God's Son!"

The peace of Christ go with you.

And also with you. Amen.

Year C

In this week of holy preparation, let us join all Jesus' friends,
including the women who had followed him from Galilee,
to watch these things and wait for the dawn of God's new day.

The peace of Christ go with you.

And also with you. Amen.

PART TWO

The Sundays
of Easter

Introduction

The gift of Jesus' resurrection is eternal life, starting with the joy of abundant life now as the one body of Jesus Christ. We often celebrate the birthday of the church on Pentecost, but, of course, the church begins already with the resurrection and with Jesus' immediate instructions to Mary Magdalene and the other disciples to go and proclaim that he has risen. In John's Gospel a group of gathered disciples receives the Spirit from Jesus on the evening of Easter Day and are soon invited by Jesus to witness and to care for the flock. All humanity, indeed all creation, is to be offered the life-giving power of Jesus' resurrection. We celebrate Pentecost Day for the coming of the Spirit on a large group of the faithful, an astonishing event that broke divisive barriers of language and ethnicity and gave to those gathered, and consequently to us, the power to witness by our words and works. This story is part of the Easter message. Pentecost, in fact, is one of the Sundays of Easter, the Fiftieth Day, the day that closes the Easter season.

Jesus' ascension is also part of the resurrection story, as we sing in the Philippians hymn: Jesus leaves God's throne, humbles himself, is born in human likeness, and becomes obedient to death on the cross: "Therefore God also highly exalted him and gave him a name that is above every name" (2:9). Today's congregations, finding it difficult to schedule an Ascension Day service on Thursday, the fortieth day after Easter, may celebrate the feast on the nearest Sunday. But Ascension is an integral part of the Easter celebration. As we hear again in John's Gospel, Jesus' words connect the ascension and resurrection events. Jesus says to Mary Magdalene at the tomb: "Do not hold on to me, because I have not yet ascended to the Father. But go to my brothers and say to them, 'I am ascending to my Father and your Father, to my God and your God'" (John 20:17).

The ascension is thus part of the formation of the church. Jesus tells the disciples, who will witness Jesus being taken into heaven, to rejoice because he is returning to God's right hand and sending them the Spirit by which they will receive the power to do mighty works in his name (John 14:28). At the same time, because Jesus is the One who descended to share our human suffering and weakness, Jesus takes our pain and limitations with him and transforms them: "When he ascended on high, he made captivity itself a captive; he gave gifts to his people" (Ephesians 4:8). Charles Wesley's hymn "Hail the Day That Sees Him Rise" pictures Jesus ascending to heaven with unending love for the earth he leaves, and as Jesus ascends, he bestows "blessings on his church below."

We are therefore celebrating during the whole of the Easter season the resurrection of Jesus Christ, the stone who was rejected and yet became the chief cornerstone, and at the same time celebrating the power of resurrection in the life of the church today, which includes taking the word of life to the world. The eight Sundays of Easter flow from the resurrection narrative read on Easter Day and the joyous celebration that comes with its reading. Our music, drama, visual art, prayers, proclamation, and sacramental celebrations will be the best that we can offer to honor the Lord of life, and one day is not enough. The laughter and dancing, the singing and the Alleluias extend over Fifty Days of Jubilee.

Each Sunday in Easter discloses more about our resurrected Lord and the God who sent him so that the world might have life. If we know Jesus, we know the One who sent him: "Whoever has seen me has seen the Father. . . . Do you not believe that I am in the Father and the Father in me?" (John 14:9-10). Those who use the Revised Common Lectionary follow a design in the progression of the narratives chosen for this season. The risen Jesus is revealed on the first three Sundays of Easter through stories of the disciples who saw him alive and ate and drank with him. On the fourth and fifth Sundays we hear several of Jesus' "I AM" statements from John: "I am the good shepherd," "I am the gate," "I am the true vine," "I am the way, the truth, and the life," and, from Revelation, "I am the Alpha and Omega." These statements remind us of the many ways Jesus continues to relate to us and open the door of life to us. They also emphasize that Jesus is one with the God of Israel, the same God who heard the cries of the people who were Pharaoh's slaves and told Moses to lead them out of Egypt by the decree of the God whose name is "I AM" (Exodus 3:14).

The sixth and seventh Sundays focus on Jesus' words to the disciples about his ascension and the coming of the Holy Spirit. On the seventh Sunday Jesus' prayer in John 17 relates his oneness with God to oneness with the community of faith he leaves behind. We hear what Jesus said to his disciples, and by extension to the church, about glorifying God, about abiding in Jesus as Jesus abides in God and God in him. As part of the Easter celebration, then, we learn that new life means an invitation to live in the community of God, the resurrection household. God and Jesus by their love, and by the power of the Holy Spirit, bring us into their most intimate relationship. In the Easter readings from 1 Peter, 1 John, and Revelation, we hear these themes amplified as they were disclosed in the letters to new churches that the early missionaries had started.

On all the Sundays of Easter the stories of the early growth of the church in Acts introduce us to the impassioned preaching of the apostles in a variety of cultural contexts, the power of the resurrection to heal and unite, and the establishment of communities that ate and prayed together and cared for the poor. We see how these communities thrived in love, grace, and peace, even in hostile places, and how they were anointed like Jesus to preach good news to the poor, release to the captives, freedom to the oppressed, and wholeness to the sick and disabled. We read about those who suffered jail and persecution for the sake of the gospel; we hear the story of Stephen's martyrdom, how he looked into heaven and saw Jesus standing at God's right hand. All these stories guide us in our spiritual formation and impart life to our own community of faith.

A word of caution is necessary about the harm—not only potential harm but realized outrages against the Jews—that results from taking some of the words we read in Acts out of context and construing them to blame the whole Jewish people for Jesus' crucifixion. Peter's preaching in Acts 2:22-32 (Second Sunday of Easter, Revised Common Lectionary, Year A) needs particular care and study in this regard. Verse 23 has too often served to incite hatred and should be left out of the reading in worship unless those who hear it are adequately prepared. Verse 29, on the other hand, makes clear that Peter himself was an Israelite, as were all Christians on the day of this sermon, and therefore the Jewish people can not be held responsible for Jesus' death, which was, after all, a Roman execution. Some of Peter's strong condemnations may arise from anxiety over the persecution of his own community and other Jewish factions by the same religious leaders who had wanted to silence Jesus. The criticism is of imbedded religious authority in all times and places that preserves its power at all costs and fears what is new and welcoming about God's word of life.

The essential message from Peter and the other early preachers is that Jesus "both died and was buried. . . . This Jesus God raised from the dead, and of that all of us are witnesses. Being therefore exalted at the right hand of God, and having received from the Father the promise of the Holy Spirit, he has poured out this that you both see and hear" (Acts 2:29*b*, 32-33). This sequence of events, viewed as one great act of God, who loves the world, is the basis for our celebration of the glorious season of Easter and for our life together every day of the year. We are united with the earth and all its creatures in the hope of the resurrection, the power of God to put our enemy death under Jesus' footstool and set all creation free from bondage and decay.

> When this perishable body puts on imperishability, and this mortal body puts on immortality, then the saying that is written will be fulfilled:
> "Death has been swallowed up in victory."
> "Where, O death, is your victory?
> Where, O death, is your sting?" . . .
> Thanks be to God, who gives us the victory through our Lord Jesus Christ.
>
> (1 Corinthians 15:54-56, 57*b*)

Easter Day

This day is an invitation to joyous Easter laughter, singing, dancing, and prayers of praise. It is the day that makes us a community of life and hope. Everything about our worship celebrates the great mystery of our faith: "Christ has died; Christ is risen, Christ will come again."

Greeting

> Alleluia! Christ is risen!
> **Christ is risen indeed! Alleluia!**

Call to Worship

> Glad songs of victory ring out
> in the tents of the righteous:

> **"The right hand of the LORD does valiantly;**
> **the right hand of the LORD is exalted."**

> I shall not die, but I shall live,
> and tell the deeds of the LORD.

> **The LORD is my strength and my might;**
> **the LORD has become my salvation.**

> Let all the people say:
> God's steadfast love endures forever.

> **God's steadfast love endures forever. Alleluia!**
> *(Based on Psalm 118:1-2, 14-24)*

Opening Prayer

> Mighty and gracious God, you raised Christ Jesus from the dead
> and raised us with him also, that we may have life in him:

Give us words to praise you and songs to sing Christ's glorious
resurrection.
Keep safe in us the witness of those who ate and drank with
their risen Lord
that we may eat and drink with him at your resurrection table.
"Christ the Lord is risen today!" Alleluia! **Amen.**

Call to Confession

"All the prophets testify about Jesus that everyone who believes
in him receives forgiveness of sins through his name." Let us
now confess our sins, assured that through Jesus' death and resurrection, we have forgiveness and life. *(Quotation based on Acts
10:43)*

Prayer of Confession

**O God, you gave your only Son to die for the sin of the world:
We confess that we often fail to hold firmly
to the message of his resurrection.
We have not responded to your love with our whole hearts;
we too often fall victim to despair and fear;
we are indifferent to the cries of the poor
and the calls for peace;
we, who should praise you every day, are strangely silent.
Take away the sting of death
and put within us your victory for life.
In Jesus' name. Amen.**

Words of Assurance

"For I handed on to you as of first importance what I in turn
had received: that Christ died for our sins in accordance with
the scriptures, and that he was buried, and that he was raised
on the third day in accordance with the scriptures" *(1 Corinthians
15:3-4)*. Alleluia!

Acts of Praise   *"Whom Do You Seek?"*

*Liturgical drama was used in the Middle Ages to focus the com-
munity on the significance of the feast day. An early example of*

this use of drama is the Quem Quaeritis? *(Whom do you seek?)
which was probably first presented by monks at Easter matins.
In our Easter worship settings, it is appropriate to present this
brief drama immediately before the reading of the Easter
Gospel. There are only three lines of dialogue and the action is
simple. Two actors in white robes stand on the center steps to
the chancel. Three actors in darker robes and head coverings
enter and come slowly down the aisle, bearing jars of spices.
After the dialogue is spoken, the actors remain in tableau for a
few moments and then take their seats as the congregation
sings a familiar chorus of "Alleluia." For more on possible
ways to incorporate this drama into worship see Fredericka
Berger,* "Quem Quaeritis? A Liturgical Drama for All Time," *in
Liturgy 13:4 (Winter 1996): 1-3.*

First Angel:
Whom do you seek in the tomb, O followers of Christ?

The Three Women:
Jesus of Nazareth who was crucified, O Heavenly Messengers.

Second Angel:
He is not here; he is risen, just as he said.
Go and tell the others that he is risen from the tomb.

Hymn: **"Alleluia" or "Halle-halle-halle-lujah!"**

Prayer for Illumination

Open for us, O God, the words of the witnesses,
received by the faithful and handed on to us.
Make us free to hear and not hold back
that we may live in the joy of Jesus Christ,
crucified and risen, who calls us by our name.
Blessed be the One who comes in the name of the Lord.
Alleluia! **Amen.**

Prayer of Thanksgiving After the Offering

God of hope,
on this glad day we bring our gifts to you,

asking that they bloom like Easter flowers,
wakening the world to your gift of love.
We give thanks for the dawn of your new day,
for the rising of the Sun of righteousness,
who fills the earth with light and life.
In Jesus' name. **Amen.**

Prayers of Thanksgiving and Intercession

God, Giver of life,
you raised Jesus from the dead,
so that we, made like him, will rise like him:
"Ours the cross, the grave, the skies."
We praise you and give you thanks.

Honor and glory is yours, mighty God, now and forever.

Jesus, Son of God,
by your death and resurrection,
you overcame the rule of sin and death
to make all things new.
We praise your name above every other name.

Yours is the glory, risen, conquering Son.

Holy Jesus, you called Mary's name at the tomb
and she turned toward you;
teach us the names of those who long for your word of life.

Hear us, Lord of life.

Holy Jesus, you comforted the dying
and blessed those who mourn;
grant us grace to hear those who weep
on this day of glad songs;

Hear us, Lord of life.

Holy Jesus, you stood again among your friends;
give us courage to stand with those
who wait for justice and peace.

Hear us, Lord of life.

Holy Jesus, you work today to put our enemy death
under your footstool;
make us bearers of your light to shine out
against all threats to life.

Hear us, Lord of life.

Holy Jesus, you sent Mary to tell the good news;
now send us as witnesses,
encouraged by your Spirit of truth, united in love,
to proclaim that indeed, Christ is risen.

In the name of Jesus Christ, risen indeed. Amen.

Commission and Blessing

Those who came to mourn found an empty tomb.
Those who came weeping left dancing for joy.
Go in peace for you have found life
through Jesus Christ our Lord.
Alleluia! Glory be to God the Father,
and to the Son, and to the Holy Spirit!

God's name be praised. Alleluia!

Second Sunday of Easter

In John's Gospel Jesus comes to the disciples on Easter evening,
shows them his wounds, and gives them the Holy Spirit; along with
the gift of the Spirit comes the gift of peace.

Greeting

Grace to you and peace from the One who is and who was and who
is to come, and from Jesus Christ, the faithful witness, the firstborn
of the dead, and the ruler of the kings of the earth.

(Paraphrased from Revelation 1:4-5)

Call to Worship

Our hearts are glad, and our souls rejoice;
our bodies dwell secure.

You show us the path of life
in your presence there is fullness of joy,
in your right hand are pleasures for evermore.

Let everything that breathes praise the Lord!

Alleluia! Praise the Lord!
(Based on Psalms 16 and 150)

Opening Prayer

God of life, when it was evening on the day of resurrection,
your Son came to his disciples, and they received the Spirit:
Give us grace to know the risen Christ
and show by our lives the joy of his presence.
Breathe on us and fill us with your Spirit;
strengthen us in love that we may proclaim our Lord and our
God. **Amen.**

Call to Confession

By God's great mercy we are given a new birth into a living hope
through the Resurrection of Jesus Christ from the dead. Let us
turn away from sin and walk in the joy of new life in Christ.

Prayer of Confession

Just and faithful God, if we say we have no sin,
we deceive ourselves,
and the truth is not in us.
We know your love alone lights up the night,
and yet we are caught in the glare of distractions;
we fail to listen to those who saw Jesus and believed;
we do not live together in unity and love for one another.
Forgive and cleanse us;
keep your word in us for the sake of Jesus. Amen.

Words of Assurance

Jesus loved and freed us by his blood. Let us therefore walk in the light as Jesus is in the light and have fellowship with one another.

Acts of Praise   **Welcome, New Members**

Invite the confirmation class, all who have recently joined your congregation, and all who will be joining in the coming Sundays to come forward, along with their sponsors, for welcoming and a blessing. If possible, have a small gift, such as a loaf of homemade bread, to present to each one after the hymn. If time allows, say their names to the congregation.

Pastor or lay leader: Jesus said, "I am the vine, you are the branches. Those who abide in me and I in them bear much fruit, because apart from me you can do nothing. . . . Abide in my love. . . . I have said these things to you so my joy may be in you, and that your joy may be complete."

(John 15:5, 9b, 11)

We welcome you into our community of faith where we are all God's children and therefore all brothers and sisters. We support each other and strengthen each other like the intertwining branches of a vine. We abide in the love of Jesus, the true vine, and we are cared for by God, the vine grower. We welcome you as friends of Jesus and invite you to join our ministry of making disciples and serving Christ among our neighbors.
Let us pray:

Gracious God, in your goodness
you pour upon us the gifts of your Spirit:
Prepare us for the service of your gospel.
Fill us with love for the world
that we may, like Jesus, anointed with your Spirit,
feed the hungry, free the oppressed, visit the prisoners,
bring your healing to the sick, and comfort the grieving.
Hear the prayers of our new friends,
who come to us ready to do your work.

Teach us to offer your hospitality and caring,
and make us all at home in your love.
Bless our common ministry
that your name may be glorified.
In Jesus' name. **Amen.**

Let us join hands as we sing.

Hymn Suggeston: **"Blest Be the Tie That Binds"**

Prayer for Illumination

We do not ask, holy Jesus,
to touch or see your wounds
but that you come to us in our fear
and let us hear the words of those
who saw you and believed.
You blessed those who have not seen but yet believed:
Bless us now and take away our doubt. **Amen.**

Prayer of Thanksgiving After the Offering

Give us courage, O God, to lay at your feet our possessions,
mindful that there are those among us who are needy.
Show us how to live with less and love you more.
Strengthen in us the faith that is more precious than gold,
and we will sing our thanksgiving to you in joy forever.
In Jesus' name. **Amen.**

Prayers of Thanksgiving and Intercession

God of glory, your word declares to us from the beginning
that you raised Jesus up
and exalted him to be our leader and friend:
Fill us with your gladness.
Show us how to love Jesus and believe in him.

Bless us with life forever more.

Show us the path to life and the pleasant ways of peace.

Bless us with life forever more.

Show us how to live so that no one among us will be needy.

Bless us with life forever more.

We give thanks for those who saw you in their midst,
touched you with their hands,
and kept alive your word of light.
Strengthen our communion with all the saints;
join us together in the circle of Jesus' friends
that we may live in love with you and all creation.

Bless us with life for evermore.

Protect us by your power;
bring us by the Holy Spirit into fellowship with your Son;
keep us for the inheritance that is imperishable,
undefiled, and unfading:
the eternal life made ours by Jesus' resurrection.
In his name we pray.

Bless us with life for evermore. Amen.

Commission and Blessing

Behold, how good and pleasant it is when we live together in unity! Let us go in peace, made one by the Spirit in communion with the God of our ancestors and Jesus Christ, whom God raised from the dead. To Jesus Christ be all glory and honor. Alleluia! Amen!

Alleluia! Amen!

Third Sunday of Easter

This Sunday we focus on Jesus' appearances to the disciples after the resurrection during which he ate with them and commissioned them to tell others and care for his people. The witnesses who reported Jesus' eating and drinking with them give joyous cause for celebration that Jesus is alive and interacting with others "in the flesh."

Greeting

> Thanks be to God. Alleluia!
> Let every creature in heaven and on earth and under the earth
> and in the sea, and all that is in them, be heard singing,
>   "To the One seated on the throne and to the Lamb: blessing
>   and honor and glory and might for ever and ever!"
>
> *(Based on Revelation 5:13)*

Call to Worship

> Sing praises to the LORD, O you faithful ones,
> and give thanks to God's holy name.
>
> **Let the light of your face shine on us, O LORD!**
> **You have put gladness in our heart.**
>
> You have turned our mourning into dancing;
> you have taken off our sackcloth
> and clothed us with joy.
>
> **Let our souls praise you and not be silent.**
> **O LORD, our God, we will give thanks to you forever.**
>
> *(Based on Psalms 4 and 30)*

Opening Prayer

> Gracious God, you made known the risen Christ
>   in the taste of the bread he broke, the sound of his voice,
>   the imprint of his wounds, the sight of his face,
>   and the smell of breakfast cooking on the beach:

Show us through all our senses
   the new life Christ brings to us this day
   and lead us by your Spirit to welcome him with all our being,
   for the sake of the peace he came to give. **Amen.**

Call to Confession

Through Jesus Christ we have come to trust in God, who raised
Jesus from the dead and gave him glory, so that our faith and
hope are set on God. And now friends, let us repent, and turn
to God, who will wipe out our sins.

(Based on 1 Peter 1:21 and Acts 3:17)

Prayer of Confession

**Merciful God, you call us to repentance and forgiveness
through the death and resurrection of your Son Jesus Christ:
Help us to hear your call with the eagerness of the disciples;
turn us away from all distractions that keep us from seeing
Jesus and knowing who he is;
forgive us when we neglect to study the scriptures
   and fail to seek your word of life;
forgive us when we do not respond to your call
   to feed your sheep.
Help us to live as your beloved children now,
   and clothe us with joy.
In the name of Jesus, the holy and righteous One. Amen.**

Words of Assurance

The Lord's anger is but for a moment; God's favor lasts a lifetime. We have been born anew, not of perishable but of imperishable seed, through the living and enduring word of God.

(Based on Psalm 30 and 1 Peter 1:23)

Acts of Praise   **Gone Fishing**
                 An Introduction to John 21:1-19

*This brief drama for five characters and a narrator requires no
scenery or props, and the actors are dressed in something simple like warm-up suits. They move during the scene from their*

original positions on the center steps to the "boat," and finally to the "beach." The narrator, dressed in an alb or choir robe, stands at the lectern. As the scene opens the five characters are sitting on the central chancel steps looking dazed and somewhat at a loss.

Narrator: Pete, Tom, Nate, Mary, and Sally are sitting around with nothing to do.

Pete: (rising) I'm going fishing. I don't know what's happening. I don't know what I'm supposed to do, so I'm going fishing.

(They walk to an imaginary boat, climb in, sit down, and begin to row. All sing the chorus of "Michael Row the Boat Ashore." They stop rowing, drop an anchor overboard, bait their fishing lines, and throw them out, all on one side of the boat—all in pantomime—and sit in silence for a few moments.)

Pete: You got a bite yet, Tom?

Tom: No. What about you, Mary?

Mary: No. Anybody?

All: No. No. No.

Nate: I never thought it would be like this.

Mary: This isn't what he wants us to do.

Tom: I'm starving.

Sally: (sarcastically) You and about 50 million others.

Tom: Not that kind of starving, just hungry for something.

Pete: (sniffs the air) What's that I smell?

Mary: Breakfast cooking on the beach.

Nate: (as if shouting to someone on shore) What's that? *(pause; listening)* Try casting on the other side? *(They all shift their lines to the other side of the "boat" and immediately get bites. Pantomime struggling to reel fish in.)*

Mary: (stops) I know that voice.

(Pete stands up, quickly pulls off his warm-up pants, revealing swim trunks underneath, jumps overboard, and "swims" to shore. The others follow quickly, rowing the boat. They get out, hug each other, sit down on the ground, sing a blessing— The Doxology or a table grace—happily talk to each other, and eat a meal in pantomime.)

Narrator: Jesus served them again, just as he had done before, and they were full. Then Jesus looked straight at Peter and asked him, three times, if he loved him.

Pete: (stands up and faces the congregation, looking upward) Lord, you know everything; you know that I love you. *(pause; listening)* Feed your sheep?

Sally: (stands) All those hungry people.

Tom: (stands) All those fish we caught!

Mary and Nate: (stand) The hungry will be filled with good things.

Narrator: Jesus, at the wedding feast in Cana, revealed his glory by turning gallons of water into an abundance of good wine. Jesus, on the mountainside, blessed bread and broke it to feed the five thousand as much as they wanted and still gathered up twelve basketfuls left over. Jesus, risen from the dead, finds his disciples fishing and fills their net until it will hold no more. Jesus gives them food for their hungry, tired bodies and gives them himself, the bread of life. Whoever comes to Jesus will never be hungry.

"But there are also many other things that Jesus did; if every one of them were written down, I suppose that the world itself could not contain the books that would be written."

(John 21:25)

Hymn Suggestion: **"Thine Is the Glory"** *(or another resurrection hymn)*

(The actors keep their positions and sing, walking out the center aisle during the last stanza.)

Prayer for Illumination

> *Year A*
> God our teacher,
> open the scriptures to us;
> let us hear all that was told about Jesus Christ
> that we may know him, risen from the dead,
> and go out to tell of his love.
> In his name we pray. **Amen.**

> *Year B*
> God of the prophets,
> it was written that Christ must suffer
> and on the third day rise from the dead:
> Open our minds to the scriptures
> that we may see the ancient words fulfilled
> and proclaim your healing power.
> In Jesus' name. **Amen.**

> *Year C*
> Mighty God,
> Jesus called out in the dawn, and Peter jumped from the boat;
> you stopped Saul's journey of death with a light from heaven:
> Wake us up now to your word, the lamp of truth,
> that we may know you as our Lord.
> Stay with us till our eyes are opened
> and we see you in the risen Christ. **Amen.**

Prayer of Thanksgiving After the Offering

> God of all creation,
> we offer our thanksgiving and praise for your gifts
>   that come to us with overflowing abundance.
> Give us the same generosity of spirit we find in you
>   so that prosperity may extend throughout the earth.
> In the name of Jesus our Lord. **Amen.**

Prayers of Thanksgiving and Intercession

> God of Abraham, and God of Mary Magdalen
> you have glorified your servant Jesus, the Author of life.

You have promised to bring us through the night of weeping
   to the joy of the morning.
Hear our prayer for your grieving people:

For those grieving for loved ones who have died,
for those who live in fear of war,
for those in despair and those who are dying,
for those who have left the comfort of home,
for those who have lost jobs,
for those saddened by broken relationships,
Lord in your mercy,

hear our prayer.

God our healer, your apostles proclaimed faith in Jesus' name
and praised your power to make us strong and whole.
Hear our prayer for your people
and bathe them with your peace:

For the sick and those who care for them,
for victims of violence, oppression, terror, and abuse,
for friends in conflict and families in distress,
for prisoners and those trapped by failure,
for children without parents and all who are lonely,
Lord in your mercy,

hear our prayer.

God of abundant grace,
hear our prayer for all your people;
reveal in us the love you have given us,
for we are called children of God
and must be known by our love.
Free us from the old ways, help us hear you call,
open our eyes, fill our nets;
give us grace to love you more and feed your sheep.
Teach us to love one another deeply from the heart
and live in mutual love and obedience to your truth.
Lord in your mercy,

hear our prayer.

In communion with the faithful who have died,
precious in your sight,

and in praise of your steadfast promise
that when Jesus is revealed,
we will be like him and see him as he is,
we give you thanks for your Son Jesus Christ,
the resurrection and the life.
May Jesus Christ be praised! Alleluia!

Alleluia! May Jesus Christ be praised. Amen.

Commission and Blessing

We are new creations in Christ:
Send us, O Lord, to serve you as your hosts above.
Make us ready to join the myriads of myriads,
and thousands of thousands,
who sing with full voice before your throne:
"Worthy is the Lamb."

Alleluia! Bless the Lord.

The Lord's name be praised. Alleluia! Amen.

Fourth Sunday of Easter

This Sunday is often called Good Shepherd Sunday because the traditional readings are from John 10 and Psalm 23. The image of Jesus as shepherd is still comforting, even to those of us who live in urban settings, and it carries additional meaning from Old Testament associations of a righteous ruler who cares for the needs of the people.

Greeting

For this reason we are before the throne of God: to worship God day and night. The One seated on the throne will shelter us; the Lamb at the center of the throne will be our shepherd. The Lamb will guide us to the water of life, and God will wipe every tear from our eyes. Come, let us worship the Lord!

(Based on Revelation 7:15, 17)

Call to Worship

Praise to the Lord our shepherd,
who gives us all we need for life.

**We are fed in green pastures;
we are washed in the calm waters of God's goodness.**

God leads us on the path to life
and comforts us in the darkest valley.

**The Lord spreads a table for us before our enemies
and anoints us with healing oil.**

The cup of God's blessing overflows for us;
God restores our life.

**We will dwell in God's house our whole life long.
Alleluia!** *(Based on Psalm 23)*

Opening Prayer

God, our Shepherd and Ruler, you give us life and joy;
   you know our names and provide for us all that we need:
Teach us to trust in you alone and listen for your voice.
Guide us in the teachings of your apostles,
   who devoted themselves to breaking bread and prayers.
May we, like them, be surrounded by the goodwill of others
   and praise your name in acts of love.
In the name of Jesus Christ, crucified and risen. **Amen.**

Call to Confession

When we, like sheep, go astray, our Shepherd calls us and we know his voice. Let us confess our sin and return to the Shepherd and guardian of our souls.

Prayer of Confession

**Merciful God,
when we stray from your ways and listen to other voices,**

you find us and bring us back:
    forgive us when we cling to possessions
        and neglect those in need;
    forgive us when we fail to act for the good of all;
    forgive us when we hesitate to welcome those from another fold.
Help us to stand before you as one flock,
    healed by Jesus' wounds,
    and trusting in his name alone. Amen.

Words of Assurance

God, who is greater than our own conscience, does not condemn us. Jesus himself carried our sins in his body to the tree, so that free from sins, we might live together in love for one another. Thanks be to God.

Acts of Praise   **The Singing of Psalm 23**

Ask the children or youth to lead the congregation in reciting Psalm 23 and then singing one of the metrical versions of the psalm. "The Lord's My Shepherd, I'll Not Want" from the Scottish Psalter is the best known, but also familiar are "The King of Love My Shepherd Is" (Henry Williams Baker) and "My Shepherd Will Supply My Need" (Isaac Watts). There are also newer musical settings if resources outside the hymnals are available.

Prayer for Illumination

Savior, lead us like a shepherd to quiet pastures
    where we can hear your voice.
Show us where we can drink from deep pools
    and eat from your table.
Revive us by your Spirit
    and come toward us with your goodness.
In Jesus' name. **Amen.**

Prayer of Thanksgiving After the Offering

Give us glad and generous hearts, O God:
generous enough to provide for those who have need,
and glad enough to praise forever the name of the One

who came to give us life, and give it abundantly.
To Jesus Christ be all glory and honor. **Amen.**

Prayers of Thanksgiving and Intercession

God of love, you sent Jesus to be the good shepherd
who lays down his life for his sheep:
Keep us faithful in the name of your Son Jesus Christ.

God has given us the Spirit of truth:
Help us to love one another as Jesus loves us.

You love us so perfectly that we need not fear:
Give us courage to endure all hardship
in remembrance of Christ's suffering.

Our Shepherd cares for us with goodness and mercy:
Teach us to respond with acts of charity and goodwill.

Your apostles lived with all things in common,
breaking bread and praying together:
Make us a community of love.

God's love abides in us as it abides in Jesus:
Teach us to show our love in truth and in action.

You gave your apostles power to heal in your name,
that all may stand before you in good health:
Help us to bring your healing power to all creation.

We are healed by our Savior's wounds:
Teach us to safeguard and enjoy our abundant life.

You sent Jesus to be the gate to your fold
who keeps out evil and opens the way for us to go in:
Protect us and welcome us home.

The Good Shepherd calls us by our name:
Give us grace to follow and give thanks.

In the name of Jesus Christ of Nazareth,
whom God raised from the dead. **Amen.**

Commission and Blessing

Amen! Blessing and glory and wisdom
and thanksgiving and honor

and power and might
be to our God forever and ever! Amen. *(Revelation 7:12)*

The peace of our Lord Jesus Christ go with you. Alleluia!

And also with you. Alleluia!

Fifth Sunday of Easter

The image of the vine with its intertwining branches, the promise of the resurrection household with many rooms, the new commandment to love one another as Jesus loves us: these are all part of the preparation Jesus gives his disciples for living in his abiding presence through the Holy Spirit when he has returned to the Father, and they are our watchwords for living now as Christ's body, the church.

Greeting

The One who was seated on the throne said, "See, I am making all things new. . . . I am the Alpha and the Omega, the beginning and the end. To the thirsty I will give water as a gift from the spring of the water of life." Come, let all who are thirsty receive God's gift of water and live in the love of God, the grace of Jesus Christ, and the communion of the Holy Spirit. *(Quotation from Revelation 21:5-6)*

Call to Worship

You, O God, are the source of all our praise
   in the great congregation;
we will make our promises before those who fear God:
The poor shall eat and be satisfied;
   those who seek the LORD shall give praise

All the ends of the earth shall remember and turn to the LORD;
all the families of the nations shall worship before you.
For dominion belongs to the LORD, who rules over all.

All who sleep in the earth shall bow down before God;

all who go down to the dust shall worship,
and I shall live for the LORD.

Our children will serve our God;
future generations will be told about the Lord,
saying, "The LORD has done it!" Alleluia!

(Based on Psalm 22:25-31)

Opening Prayer

God of all creation, you have promised a new heaven
   and a new earth;
   embracing this hope, we look to you for newness of life today.
We have tasted that the Lord is good,
   and we ask for courage to be your disciples:
Help us to abide in you as you abide in Christ.
Help us to grow in our love for one another
   that we may be known by our love.
Make us bearers of good fruit that glorifies your name.
All things we ask in the name of our risen Lord. **Amen.**

Call to Confession

Our times are in God's hands; let us confess our sin and ask God
to deliver us from the time of trial.

Prayer of Confession

O God, our rock of refuge and our strong fortress,
lead us to your mercy; guide us as we confess to you our sin.
You know our limitations and failures;
you have offered to cleanse us by your word:
Keep us from hurting others, causing needless conflict,
being impatient, making hasty judgments,
and forgetting those who are hungry;
cleanse us from all envy and false pride.
Let your face shine on us, O God;
save us in your steadfast love, for Jesus' sake. Amen.

Words of Assurance

"Once we were not a people, but now we are God's people;
once we had not received mercy, but now we have received

mercy." Through Jesus Christ, the chief cornerstone, we are forgiven, given life, and created a new people.

(Quotation based on 1 Peter 2:10)

Acts of Praise   **Psalm 148**

As an act of praise, ask the children's choir or a children's church school class to prepare ahead of time and act out Psalm 148. Puppets or costumes—angels, sun, stars, snowflakes, animals, for example—may be used. The children may lead the congregation in singing an appropriate song or hymn and in the responsive reading of the psalm from the hymnal or the adapted version below.

Praise the Lord! Praise the Lord from the heavens:
angels and all the heavenly hosts, sun, moon, and stars.

Praise the Lord! Praise the Lord from the earth:
mountains and hills, fruit trees and evergreens,
wild animals and cattle, creeping things and flying birds,
sea creatures, fire, hail, snow, frost, and stormy wind.

Praise the Lord, who spoke and you were created,
who established you forever and set your boundaries.

Praise the Lord, all rulers of the earth and all peoples,
young men and women alike, old and young together!
Let all God's faithful people praise the Lord!

(Based on Psalm 148)

Hymn Suggestion: **"All Things Bright and Beautiful"**

Prayer for Illumination

Year A
Free our troubled hearts, O God,
and reveal to us your marvelous light.
Bring us to the place
where we can know your Son
and your love that dwells in him.
Guide us by your truth and lead us to life.
In the name of Jesus who glorifies you. **Amen.**

Year B
God our good gardener,
strengthen us by your abiding love.
Open to us the words of Jesus
that we may learn to be his disciples.
Make us faithful branches, growing together
and bearing fruit to your glory.
In the name of Jesus, our true vine. **Amen.**

Year C
Show us your holy city, O Lord;
show us the new thing you do in our midst.
Give us grace to love as Jesus loved
and to show by our love for each other
that we are your disciples,
for you have given us the way to life.
In Jesus' name. **Amen.**

Prayer of Thanksgiving After the Offering

God our provider, we are your grateful people:
Make us servants of the poor like Stephen;
give us grace and power like his that we may see your face
and praise you in all the works we do.
We give thanks in the name of Jesus Christ,
your only Son, sent that we might have life. **Amen.**

Prayers of Thanksgiving and Intercession

Jesus, Savior, you call us to be your disciples;
you nurture and shape us into your church,
growing and loving, acting always on your behalf.

You are the vine; we are the branches.

Jesus, joy of heaven who came to earth,
live in us; make us your home.

Apart from you we can do nothing.

Show us how to lose our old life for your sake
and gain, by your grace, the life you came to give.

Apart from you we wither like a branch cut off from the vine.

Jesus, Son of God, sender of the Holy Spirit,
encourage us when we hesitate;
show us how to live in your household.

Teach us to abide in you as you abide in us.

Your commandments are new and good;
you ask us to love one another as you have loved us.

Grant us grace to keep your commandments.

You ask us to take up our cross and follow you.

Grant us grace to become your disciples.

You invite us to be known by the fruit we bear.

Grant us grace to bear much fruit for the glory of God.

You have promised us rooms in your Father's house,
a new heaven and a new earth where God wipes away all tears,
where mourning and crying and pain will be no more,
where death will be no more:
Help us to know you and know the One who sent you
that we may abide in you and live now as your new creation.

Thanks be to God for Jesus Christ, our way, our truth, our life.
May the name of Jesus Christ be forever praised. Amen.

Commission and Blessing

> Come, my Way, my Truth, my Life:
> such a way as gives us breath,
> such a truth as ends all strife,
> such a life as killeth death.
>
> *(George Herbert, 1633)*

Send us in your love, O God, strengthened by the breath of
your Spirit, sustained by the peace of Christ, and rejoicing in
your victory over death that brings abundant life to all who call
on your name. Alleluia! **Amen.**

Sixth Sunday of Easter

The focus of the sixth Sunday of Easter is anticipation of Jesus' ascension. The disciples, perplexed and fearful at Jesus' announcement that he will complete the act of resurrection and return to his place at God's side, need comfort and direction. The assurance Jesus gives is that the Advocate, the Holy Spirit, will be with them forever and teach them to remember all that Jesus has said and done.

Greeting

God opens for us the crystal fountain, the river of the water of life, flowing from the throne of God and of the Lamb. Come, let us wash in its healing stream, led by God's powerful hand.

(Based on Revelation 22:1 and "Guide Me, O Thou Great Jehovah")

Call to Worship

May God be gracious to us and bless us;
make your face to shine upon us, O God,
that your way may be known upon earth,
your saving power among all nations.

**Let the peoples praise you, O God;
let all the peoples praise you.**

Let the nations be glad and sing for joy,
for you judge the peoples with equity
and guide the nations upon earth.

**Let the peoples praise you, O God;
let all the peoples praise you. Alleluia!**

(Based on Psalm 67:1-5)

Opening Prayer

God our deliverer,
you raised your Son Jesus from the dead,
    and now he calls us his friends:
Show us the way to live in love and friendship with all earth's
    people.

Help us to bring your gift of peace wherever conflict reigns.
Make us ready to receive your Spirit of truth,
  our companion and guide,
  and lead us into the light of your glory
  to join those who bring you the honor of the nations.
In the name of Jesus Christ, risen and glorified. **Amen.**

Call to Confession

We are always eager to do what is good, but even when we fail, we have an Advocate who will help us keep God's word and will intercede for us when we approach the throne of grace. Let us therefore confess our sin.

Prayer of Confession

God of grace, we know that if your love abides in us,
we will keep your commandment to love one another:
   We are troubled that we are not always faithful to your word;
   we are afraid that we will fail as bearers of your gift of peace;
   we are worried that we do not know you as we ought;
   we are anxious and hold back from embracing others in your love.
Take away our fear and lead us by your Spirit to the healing stream.
Abide in us as you abide in Jesus, in whose name we pray. Amen.

Words of Assurance

"For Christ also suffered for sins once for all, the righteous for the unrighteous, in order to bring us to God." In the name of Jesus Christ, whom God raised from the dead, we are forgiven.

(Quotation from 1 Peter 3:18a)

Acts of Praise   *Psalm 98 with Musical Instruments*

Psalm 98 presents an opportunity to ask those in the congregation who play musical instruments to participate in an act of praise. A guitar and a trumpet are especially appropriate, but other instruments are fine too. Children may be given rhythm instruments to play and everyone should be encouraged to clap when directed. A strong "conductor" is needed and a run-through just before worship begins is helpful. Below is a suggestion for incorporating music into the reading of the psalm. The final phrase of the hymn, "Sing Praise to God Who Reigns Above" may be played by a solo instrument as a fanfare between psalm verses or the words may be sung as a response by the congregation. Making a joyful noise is the goal rather than musical virtuosity.

Hymn Suggestion: **"Sing Praise to God Who Reigns Above,"**
stanzas 1 and 2

O sing to the LORD a new song,
for God has done marvelous things.

Sung or played: TO GOD ALL PRAISE AND GLORY.

God's right hand and holy arm have gained the victory.
All the ends of the earth have seen the victory of our God.

Sung or played: TO GOD ALL PRAISE AND GLORY.

Make a joyful noise to the LORD, all the earth;
break forth into joyous song and sing praises.

Sung or played: TO GOD ALL PRAISE AND GLORY.

Sing praises to the LORD with the lyre,
with the lyre and the sound of melody.

Sung or played: TO GOD ALL PRAISE AND GLORY.

With trumpets and the sound of the horn
make a joyful noise before the Sovereign, the LORD.

Sung or played: TO GOD ALL PRAISE AND GLORY.

Let the sea roar, and all that fills it;
the world and those who live in it.

*Hand clapping and playing of rhythm instruments,
continuing through the next four lines.*

Let the floods clap their hands;
let the hills sing together for joy
at the presence of the LORD,
who is coming to judge the earth.

Sung or played: TO GOD ALL PRAISE AND GLORY.

All: **O sing to the LORD a new song,
for God has done marvelous things.**

(Based on Psalm 98)

Hymn Suggestion: **"Sing Praise to God Who Reigns Above,"** *stanzas 3 and 4*

Prayer for Illumination

Year A
God, you invite us into the abiding love
that enfolds you and your Son Jesus Christ:
Help us to keep Jesus' commandments;
prepare us to give an account of the hope that is in us
with all gentleness and reverence.
In the name of Jesus who loves us
and reveals himself to us. **Amen.**

Year B
God our teacher,
open to us the commandments Jesus gave;
help us receive them with joy
and turn them into acts of love.
Guide us by your Spirit of truth
that we may know you and abide in your love.
In the name of Jesus, our friend. **Amen.**

Year C
Keep us faithful to your word, O God;
give us grace to show our love for you.
Make your home with us, and keep us from fear;
open us to receive your Spirit,
the One who will teach us everything
in remembrance of Jesus, risen and ascended. **Amen.**

Prayer of Thanksgiving After the Offering

> God of grace and glory, you have shown us
>> that our praise of you is useless if we forget the poor:
> Take our gifts and hear us accept your charge to live
>> so that all in need will be satisfied.
> Now welcome our praise, and we will glorify your name,
>> for the sake of your Son who abides in you. **Amen.**

Prayers of Thanksgiving and Intercession

> Praise to God, the Father of Jesus Christ,
>> who breathes the Spirit of life into us.
> Praise to Jesus Christ, our Savior,
>> who reigns forever with God and the Holy Spirit.
> Praise to the Holy Spirit,
>> sent from God in Jesus' name to be with us always.

> **May your great name be praised.**

> God, in whom we live and move and have our being,
>> you sent your only Son into the world
>> so that we might live through him:
> Help us to love one another in praise of your love
>> that excels all others.
> Surround us with the complete joy of abiding in Jesus.

> **May your great name be praised.**

> God, our Maker, you formed the world and everything in it;
>> you give us life and breath:
> Lead us to spread your love of life throughout the earth
>> so that all may live with abundant joy.
> Live in us and perfect your love in us.

> **May your great name be praised.**

> God, whose love is all compassion,
> you send us the Holy Spirit to be our Advocate and Comforter:
> Free us when we are gripped by fear of terror's cruel hand
> and captive to war's madness; help us trust you completely.
> Do not let our hearts be troubled,
>> and do not let them be afraid.

May your great name be praised.

God, we are born of you;
you keep us among the living, and do not let our feet slip:
We give you thanks for Jesus Christ,
  who came with water and the blood;
we give you thanks for the Holy Spirit,
  our teacher and sustainer.
Help us to remember our baptism and be thankful;
make us one body in Jesus Christ,
filled with the Spirit, embraced by your love.
In the name of Jesus Christ who conquers the world. Alleluia!

May your great name be praised. Alleluia! Amen.

Commission and Blessing

Jesus said, "Peace I leave with you. My peace I give to you. I do not give to you as the world gives." Let us greet each other with signs of the peace that is ours through the resurrection of Jesus Christ, who has gone into heaven and is at the right hand of God, with angels, authorities, and powers made subject to him.

(Based on John 14:27a and 1Peter 3:22)

The peace of Christ be with you.

And also with you. Alleluia! Amen.

Seventh Sunday of Easter

Throughout the Easter season and especially as we move toward Pentecost, we celebrate the beginnings of the church. This Sunday lifts up John 17, Jesus' great prayer for the people God has given him, the community of those who recognize that Jesus comes from God. Jesus prays for our unity and for our joy to be complete; as

God and Jesus, the Father and the Son, are one, so the people who share in Jesus' glory are also one in God's love.

Greeting

We are God's own people, believing in the name of Jesus Christ and sharing in Christ's glory. Let us celebrate the love of God who sent Jesus to die for us, be raised again on the third day, and ascend to reign at the right hand of God. Let us give thanks for the great unbounded love of God that makes us one with Jesus Christ as Jesus Christ is one with God. Thanks be to God. Alleluia!

Call to Worship

The LORD reigns! Let the earth rejoice
let the many coastlands be glad!
Clouds and thick darkness are all around the LORD;
righteousness and justice are the foundation of God's reign.

Sing to God, sing praises to God's name;
lift up a song to the One who rides upon the clouds;
rejoice before the One whose name is the Lord.

O Rider in the heavens, the ancient heavens:
we listen to the thunder of God's mighty voice.
Awesome is the God of Israel,
who gives power and strength to the people.

Blessed be God! Alleluia!

(Based on Psalms 98:1-2; and 67:4, 33, 35)

Opening Prayer

God of love,
we are the community of life you gave to Jesus Christ,
We thank you for the work you sent him to do.
Help us to pray together as the disciples did, waiting on the Spirit.
Help us to act in love and unity so all may know that Jesus came,
loving the world, as you love him.
Help us bring your justice to the powerless
and your care to those without resources.

In all things, we glorify your name,
for we share in the glory of Jesus your Son
in whose name we pray. **Amen.**

Call to Confession

The Lord knows everyone's heart; God knows that, like a roaring lion, our adversary prowls around us. If we turn to God in humility and sincerity, God will strengthen and forgive us. Let us cast all our anxiety on God who cares for us.

Prayer of Confession

God our strength and shield,
your face shines on those who love justice and reject evil:
Give us grace to work for your goodness
  and forsake wrongdoing;
    free us from being bound by anger and fear;
    alert us to acts that harm or exploit your children;
    teach us to discipline ourselves in love;
    stop us from doing anything that dishonors your name.
Give us courage to face the hosts of evil round us
  and the selfishness and pride that threaten us within.
Protect us in the name of Jesus, who came to give eternal life.
Amen.

Words of Assurance

By his death on the cross for our sins, Jesus was humbled and then exalted, raised from death, and given a name that is above every other name. We know also that if we humble ourselves under the mighty hand of God, God will exalt us in due time. God's name be praised.

Acts of Praise   *Give Thanks for All the Saints*

The book of Acts tells the stories of those who became disciples in the early church. Some, like Peter and Paul, are well known, but others are unnamed or have minor roles that we often neglect in telling the story. What follows is a reading that lifts up some of the disciples we may have forgotten and offers thanks for their gifts to us. It can be used as written as a responsive reading or expanded into a series of short monologues, with members of the congregation assigned to portray each character. The actors will study the Acts readings ahead of time and prepare a brief statement in their own words to deliver with the prayer that illuminates the work and identity of their character.

Leader: The diverse group of disciples who shared all things in common—breaking bread and praying together, taking care of those in need, and telling everyone about the death and resurrection of Jesus Christ—formed the community that we know as the first church. We hear their stories in the book of Acts; some are famous, others remain obscure. Let us thank God for all the saints, including those who could not preach like Peter or pray like Paul but, led by the Spirit, told the love of Jesus and lived lives of hope that still bless us today.

For Mary, Jesus' mother, who joined the community in prayer
and waited with them for the Spirit, *(Acts 1:12-14)*

we give you thanks, O God.

For Matthais, who became the new apostle
and witnessed to the resurrection, *(Acts 1:21-26)*

we give you thanks, O God.

For the Ethiopian official, who came from far away, searched
the Scriptures, was found by Philip, and asked to be baptized,
(Acts 8:26-40)

we give you thanks, O God.

For Ananias, who was not afraid to care for Paul in his need,
to bring him healing and teach him the way of Christ,
(Acts 9:10-19a)

we give you thanks, O God.

For Dorcas, who was loved for her acts of charity and goodwill and whom Peter raised up from death in Jesus' name,
(Acts 9:36-42)

we give you thanks, O God.

For Cornelius, the Roman centurion, who feared God and persevered until Peter came and baptized in his house,

(Acts 10:1-48)

we give you thanks, O God.

For Lydia, the businesswoman, who was judged to be faithful to the Lord and opened her home in Philippi to Paul and Silas,

(Acts 16:11-15)

we give you thanks, O God.

For Silas, Paul's traveling companion, who endured jail and earthquakes and continued to sing hymns to God,

(Acts 16:16-34)

we give you thanks, O God.

For the other witnesses, named and unnamed, who heard God's word and suffered for the sake of the Gospel: we give thanks that they were led by the Holy Spirit to keep alive for us the testimony of Jesus' death and resurrection.

For all the saints, by whom our lives are blessed,
we give you thanks, O God. Amen.

Hymn Suggestion: ***"For All the Saints"***

Prayer for Illumination

> God of all grace,
> help us to hear Jesus' astounding word of love
> that brings us into the glorious community
> where you live with him and the Holy Spirit.
> Open us to the gift of life, eternal and abundant,
> whereby we know you, the only true God,
> and Jesus Christ whom you have sent.
> Make us worthy of your glory,
> in the name of Jesus Christ. **Amen.**

Prayer of Thanksgiving After the Offering

God, you are the source of all our gifts,
we praise you and thank you for the joy of hospitality,
the pleasure of feeding the hungry in your name,
the delight of sharing the gifts of abundant life.
Prepare us to feast in gladness at your table,
abiding forever with you and all the saints.
In the name of Jesus Christ, ascended and glorified. **Amen.**

Prayers of Thanksgiving and Intercession

God of glory, your Son Jesus came down to live with us
    and died on the cross to give us eternal life.
This same Jesus, you raised from the dead and brought again
    on high.
Teach us not to gaze toward the heavens in sadness and fear
but to rejoice that he has gone to you and sends us the Spirit.
Give us grace to face the troubles of the world with courage,
assured that if we share in Jesus' sufferings,
we will shout for joy when he comes again, revealed in glory.

Wake us up to the needs of your people.
Keep us in remembrance of Jesus' words of blessing,
and prepare us to accept his charge to go to all the world
with words and deeds of love, for the glory of his name.

Send us in love, O God, that the world may believe.

Guide us to comfort the grieving for the sake of Jesus' sorrow,
to visit the prisoners, singing hymns with Paul and Silas,
to care for the sick as the apostles healed in your name,
to give food and shelter, remembering those who welcomed
    your disciples.

Deliver those in distress and embrace those who suffer.

Redeem all governments and rulers from war and hatred.
Free all people to come and go in peace.
Lead us to your tree of life,
whose leaves are for the healing of the nations.
Make us caretakers of the earth, that all creation may thrive.

Establish justice and peace in all creation.

Strengthen your church, secure in your word of life;
make us one body in the love of Jesus who abides in you.
Give us grace to wash our robes in remembrance of our baptism,
that we may be ready to walk in your holy city,
singing praises with the saints to the One
who makes all things new.

Bring us all to share in your eternal reign of joy and peace.

The grace of the Lord Jesus be with all the saints. **Amen.**

Commission and Blessing

Jesus Christ, who is the root and descendant of David, the
bright and morning star, the Alpha and the Omega, the first
and the last, the beginning and the end, will bless us with life.
The God of all grace who has called us to eternal glory in
Christ will restore, support, strengthen, and establish us.

(Based on Revelation 22:13, 16b; 1 Peter 5:10)

To God be glory forever and ever.

Alleluia! Amen.

Day of Pentecost

Greeting

In the beginning, the wind of God's Spirit
swept across the face of the waters,
bringing all creation into being.
On the day of Pentecost, the fire of God's Spirit
came storming down on the disciples,
a gift from Jesus to seal them in the glory of his cross.
On this day, by the Holy Spirit's power, we are one people,

given life through Jesus' death and resurrection.
Let us praise the Lord! Alleluia!

Call to Worship

Praise to the LORD who creates in abundance!
O LORD, in wisdom you made all your works;
the earth is full of your creatures.

**You send forth your Spirit, and they are created;
you renew the face of the ground.**

May the glory of the LORD endure forever;
may the LORD rejoice in all creation;
the LORD, who looks on the earth and it trembles,
who touches the mountains and they smoke.

**I will sing to the LORD as long as I live;
I will sing praise to my God while I have being.**

Bless the LORD, O my soul.

Praise the LORD!

(Based on Psalm 104:24, 30-33, 35 b)

Opening Prayer

Mighty God,
at Pentecost you poured out your Spirit on the disciples
and opened the way of eternal life to every nation
    under heaven:
Send us abroad with the gifts given to us by the Spirit,
that by the preaching of the gospel
and by deeds of truth and love,
your Holy Spirit may reach the ends of the earth.
Glorify us in your name
and make rivers of the water of life flow from our hearts,
    through Jesus Christ our Lord. **Amen.**

Call to Confession

We have an Advocate with God, the Holy Spirit, who inter-
cedes for us with sighs too deep for words. Let us, with the
Spirit's help, bring to God our sins and cares.

Prayer of Confession

> O God, when Jesus ascended into heaven,
> he promised that we would not be alone:
> Give us grace to know your presence
> when we are troubled and afraid.
> We confess that we do not always follow your Spirit's
> guidance;
> we have neglected to use the gifts made ours by the Spirit's
> power;
> we often fail to love your children as the Spirit has taught
> us.
> Make us new by the boldness of your Holy Spirit,
> and guide us to share our gifts for the common good.
> Help us live in peace for the sake of Christ who left his peace.
> In the name of Jesus Christ. Amen.

Words of Assurance

> Paul reminds us that "in the one Spirit we were all baptized
> into one body—Jews or Greeks, slaves or free—and we were all
> made to drink of one Spirit" *(1 Corinthians 12:13)*. By our baptism
> in the Holy Spirit, we know that God has forgiven us and made
> us free. Thanks be to God.

Acts of Praise **Circle of Wind and Fire, Circle of Love**

> *For this dramatization, ask the youth group to prepare ahead
> of time and act as the leaders who form the circle and make the
> motions. The props needed are strips of red cloth, about 18
> inches long and 4 inches wide. The strips of cloth will first be
> held by each participant in the circle and waved in response to
> the reading. When the prayer is said, the participants stretch
> out their hands and form a connected circle by holding on to
> each other's cloths. The number of these cloths needed will
> depend on the size of the circle you plan to make. Ideally the
> circle, consisting of the participants with their arms out-
> stretched and the strips of cloths held between them, should
> surround the whole congregation. Children and others can be
> invited to join the circle to make it big enough, or in smaller*

churches, the entire congregation can participate. The leader and readers will need to rehearse with the core group of participants who will lead in the action.

Hymn Suggestion: **"Every Time I Feel the Spirit"**

During the singing, the participants move into a circle around the congregation. Each holds a red strip of cloth. Every time the response below is said, the cloths are held up and waved to simulate the motion of wind and flame. A tambourine or other rhythm instrument may also be played.

Reader: Jesus told his disciples to wait in the city for the Spirit to come from God, and they would be "clothed with power from on high." *(Luke 24:49)*

People: **Come Holy Spirit! Breathe into us the winds of new life. Kindle in us the fire of love.**

Reader: Jesus said that God would send the Advocate, the Holy Spirit, in his name to teach us everything and remind us of all that Jesus said. *(John 14:26)*

People: **Come Holy Spirit! Breathe into us the winds of new life. Kindle in us the fire of love.**

Reader: "When the day of Pentecost had come, they were all together in one place, and suddenly from heaven there came a sound like the rush of a violent wind, and it filled the entire house where they were sitting. Divided tongues, as of fire appeared among them and a tongue of fire rested on each of them." *(Acts 2:1-3)*

People: **Come Holy Spirit! Breathe into us the winds of new life. Kindle in us the fire of love.**

Reader: The apostles were led by the Spirit to witness to Jesus' resurrection and bring people from every race and nation to faith in God through Jesus Christ. Paul, even though a prisoner, made "every effort to maintain the unity of the Spirit in the bond of peace." He preached that "there is one body and one

Spirit, just as we were called to the one hope of our calling. One Lord, one faith, one baptism, one God and Father of all, who is above all and through all and in all."

(Ephesians 4:3-6, paraphrased)

People: **Come Holy Spirit! Breathe into us the winds of new life. Kindle in us the fire of love.**

Leader: Let us pray:

The participants in the circle reach out and connect with each other by holding on to the strips of cloth between them. The circle remains connected for the prayer and hymn.

God of wind and fire, you have breathed into us the new life of our risen and ascended Lord. As your Spirit anointed Jesus to heal the sick and proclaim good news to the oppressed, send us, empowered by that Spirit to bring comfort to those who suffer, release to the captives, food and drink to those who hunger and thirst. May the Holy Spirit bind us in your love and unite us in the one body of Jesus Christ our Lord. In Jesus' name. **Amen.**

Hymn Suggestion: **"Spirit of the Living God"**

Prayer for Illumination

> O God, you fill us with the Spirit of truth,
> who will teach us everything
> and guide us into all truth:
> Keep in us the memory of all that Jesus said.
> Inspire our meditation
> and let our thoughts please you, O God,
> for we rejoice in you. In Jesus' name. **Amen.**

Prayer of Thanksgiving After the Offering

> All creatures look to you, O God,
> to give them their food in due season.
> We call upon your name,
> and we are filled with good things.
> Alert us to the needs of your children everywhere;

teach us to use our gifts with joy for the good of all.
In the name of Jesus the Christ. **Amen.**

Prayers of Thanksgiving and Intercession

God, our Maker, you formed us in your own image
and breathed the breath of life into us:
Anoint us with your Spirit to proclaim life and hope.
When your face is hidden and we are dismayed,
send us the light of your Spirit to drive away the shadows
and show us the love of Jesus, the first fruits of resurrection.

Holy Spirit, Comforter:
Breathe your loving Spirit into every troubled heart.

Spirit of the living God, fill us with your love.

Holy Spirit, Spirit of truth:
Abide with us and show us Jesus and the One who sent him.

Spirit of the living God, fill us with your truth.

Holy Spirit, Counselor:
Be our witness that we are children of God,
heirs and joint heirs with Christ.

Spirit of the living God, fill us with your power.

Holy Spirit, Guardian of our memory:
Keep safe in us the remembrance of Jesus,
through word and sacrament.

Spirit of the living God, fill us with your hope.

Holy Spirit, Teacher:
Renew our love of your church, and teach us how to serve.

Spirit of the living God, fill us with your word.

Holy Spirit, Advocate:
Bring us understanding
that we may live in peace with all races and nations.

Spirit of the living God, fill us with your peace.

Pour your Spirit on us, O God, for the living of these days.
Give our sons and daughters courage to prophesy;

give old and young alike visions of your rule of peace.
With all of creation we wait for Jesus to return in glory,
the eternal Sovereign of heaven, come down to reign on earth.
By the sending forth of your Spirit, bind us in love
and renew the face of the earth.
In the name of Jesus our Lord. **Amen.**

Commission and Blessing

By the power of the Holy Spirit,
we confess that Jesus Christ is Lord
and proclaim the word and works of God,
who pours the Spirit on us and our descendants,
like water on the thirsty land,
blessing us with life forevermore.
Alleluia!

The peace of our Lord Jesus Christ, the love of God, and the communion of the Holy Spirit be with us all. **Amen.**

PART THREE

*Feasts and
Holy Days*

Ash Wednesday

Preparing for Ash Wednesday

Each newborn servant of the crucified
bears on the brow the seal of him who died.

George William Kitchin and Michael Robert Newbolt,
"Lift High the Cross"

Where do the ashes used for Ash Wednesday come from? The custom since at least the twelfth century is to use ashes made from burning palm branches that were given to worshipers for the Palm Sunday procession the year before. Ashes can also be bought at a religious supply store, of course, but here is one way a congregation can continue the tradition of burning last year's palms.

On Palm Sunday the worship committee or ushers collect any palms branches left behind after the procession and store them in a safe place until they are needed. Worshipers who have taken their palms home and saved them are asked to bring them back to church on the Sundays preceding Lent and place them in wicker baskets at the door of the sanctuary. On the Sunday before Ash Wednesday a group in the congregation, perhaps the senior highs and the confirmation class combined, gathers to make the ashes with the pastor and their adult leaders. Involving young people in the preparation for Ash Wednesday gives an opportunity to talk with them about the meaning of the celebration and increases their awareness of the beginning of this holy season.

The burning takes place outside at an appropriate spot on the church grounds in a brazier or a clean metal garbage can. A fire extinguisher is nearby, of course, and other precautions are planned in advance. All explanations of the process and teaching about the history of Ash Wednesday traditions should take place inside the classroom so that the burning of the palms can take place in the context of worship.

The participants form a procession and leave the church building, carrying the baskets containing palms. The leader of the procession carries a banner or the processional cross. A familiar hymn or chorus is sung during the procession and repeated as everyone gathers around the brazier and the baskets are placed on the ground in front of the group. A brief service of prayer is offered, led by young people who have prepared ahead of time. All participants will be invited to pick up a handful of palms and crumble them into the brazier at a designated time before the fire is lighted. The year-old palms will be dry and should light easily with a match. An experienced adult should do the lighting, making sure all safety precautions have been followed.

Prayers for the Burning of the Palms

Processional Hymn   **(Suggestions: "We Are Marching in the Light of God," "Lift High the Cross")**

Opening Prayer

> God of all grace,
> you bring healing and wholeness to all creation:
> Gather us in your name; light the fire of our love.
> Help us as we start the journey of Lent;
> make us ready to open our lives to you

and to remember your Son Jesus Christ
who came to set us free and give us life.
In his name. **Amen.**

Psalm

Oh, give thanks to the LORD, for the LORD is good.
God's steadfast love endures forever.

Let the people say:
God's steadfast love endures forever.

God's steadfast love endures forever.

Out of my distress I called on the LORD;
the LORD answered me and set me in a broad place.
With the LORD on my side I do not fear
What can anyone do to me?
Let the people say:
God's steadfast love endures forever.

God's steadfast love endures forever.

It is better to take refuge in the LORD
than to put confidence in human beings.
It is better to take refuge in the LORD
than to put confidence in rulers.
Let the people say:
God's steadfast love endures forever.

God's steadfast love endures forever.

I was pushed hard so that I was falling,
but the LORD has helped me.
The LORD is my strength and my might;
God has become my salvation.

Oh, give thanks to the LORD, for the LORD is good.
Let the people say:
God's steadfast love endures forever.

God's steadfast love endures forever.

(Based on Psalm 118: 1, 5-9, 13-14)

Scripture Reading   1 Peter 2:21-24   John 3:14-17

Reflection

(A few remarks on the palm leaves are offered by one of the leaders, noting that they are symbols both of Palm Sunday and Ash Wednesday and therefore of Jesus' death for the suffering world and the coming of his joyful reign. The leader asks the participants to keep a brief period of silence for reflection.)

Hymn Suggestions: **"Lord, Prepare Me to Be a Sanctuary,"**
"Spirit of the Living God"

Burning of the Palms

Leader:
Let us pray.

God of mercy, you hear the cries of the needy
    and those in distress:
Show us the hurt of those around us
and lead us to help them in your name.
As we give these palms to be burned,
we ask for the courage to leave behind past failures
and the faith to turn our lives toward you.
Renew in us our commitment to your service
that we may bring your healing to all who suffer. **Amen.**

Leader:
Let everyone in turn reach into a basket and take a handful of palms to crumble and drop into the container where they will be burned. When you come forward, you may offer a prayer, silently or out loud, for the suffering people of the world.

The leader begins by crumbling his/her palms, dropping them into the container, and saying a prayer such as the following:

"God, send your mercy to all who are homeless this day."

Others follow, and some will have prepared ahead of time to offer out loud prayers of intercession. For example:

"God, send your mercy to all who are hungry."

"God, send your mercy to all who suffer from violence or abuse."

"God, send your mercy to all whose countries are at war."

When all have had opportunity to offer prayers, the leader closes with this prayer:

Gracious God, you loved the world so much
that you sent your Son to die and rise again:
Prepare us to be marked with the ashes that signify his death
    and teach us to walk in the light of his new life.
    In Jesus' name. **Amen.**

An experienced leader lights the palms in the brazier.

Hymn Suggestions: **"Blessed Be the Name," "Seek Ye First the Kingdom of God"**

Dismissal and Blessing

    Leader:
We will return on Wednesday to receive the ashes that come from this fire. When we accept the mark of Jesus' cross on our foreheads, let us remember our baptism and be thankful.

The love of God, the grace of our Lord Jesus Christ, and the communion of the Holy Spirit be with us all. **Amen.**

The Ash Wednesday Observance

In recent years Christians from the Reformed branch of the Protestant tradition have begun to recover a practice that dates in the Western church at least to the tenth century. That is to begin Lent on the Wednesday before the First Sunday in Lent with a service of repentance and commitment, including the imposition of ashes. The Lutheran and Anglican traditions, of course, never lapsed in this observance, and the liturgical reforms of Vatican II have made Roman Catholic prayers and rubrics more accessible to other traditions through ecumenical dialogues.

One aspect of this practice that opens to us new meaning and focus is the reminder of our baptism: we receive by the water of our baptism Jesus' seal on our foreheads as we are marked by the cross of ashes at the beginning of Lent. We remember that through our baptism, "we have been united with [Christ] in a death like his" and "will be united with him in a resurrection like his" (Romans 6:5). "Remember that you are dust, and to dust you shall return" reminds us of our mortality. "Repent, and believe in the gospel" calls us to acknowledge our sin. "Remember your baptism, and be thankful" gives us reason to rejoice that in Jesus' death and resurrection, sin and death have been conquered.

The Ash Wednesday prayers of ancient origin found in newer denominational worship books bring us together ecumenically; we are unified on this day with Christians all over the world by common words and actions. Using the traditional prayers is therefore a special blessing. Even if the imposition of ashes is new to a congregation and few are expected to attend, following a pattern of worship that our ancestors in the faith used for many generations is powerful and will be enhanced if proper preparation is done ahead of time.

Beginning with a small group is not necessarily a disadvantage. In a large sanctuary with a divided chancel, a small group of worshipers can be invited to sit in the choir, facing each other to achieve more intimacy. Informal settings for Ash Wednesday observances are appropriate as well. A new experience is often less daunting if done in familiar surroundings, and informality may encourage children to participate. One possibility is to introduce a small congregation to the imposition of ashes at a service after a meal in the fellowship hall.

If a meal is served on this Wednesday, it should be simple, remembering that for many Christians this is a day of fasting. Baskets may be put on the tables to collect offerings for a food pantry or soup kitchen. If the service is to follow the meal immediately and worshipers are comfortable remaining in the same space, set up ahead of time a circle of chairs at the end of the room away from the tables.

In the center place a table holding two bowls of ashes and the cross. After supper, invite everyone to gather, leaving the dishes on the tables. Distribute orders of worship and give a few instructions so that the participants are clear about the actions and responses. Because in this setting they will impose ashes on each other, the worshipers need to be reminded of the sentence to be said— "Repent, and believe in the gospel" is one possibility—and of the method of imposition.

Once the Greeting or Call to Worship is spoken, the words and prayers should not be interrupted. After praying the Thanksgiving over the Ashes, the pastor or leader asks the worshipers to stand to receive the ashes. The leader picks up one bowl of ashes and the person assisting picks up the second. One goes to the left and one to the right, and each marks the forehead of the first person in the circle on that side. The bowls are then passed around the circle from one person to the next in both directions. When the bowls meet in the middle, the leaders stand in front of the last persons to receive the ashes and are themselves marked by those persons. In this way everyone in the room receives and everyone gives. To be marked with the cross of Christ by your neighbor, your own child, your close friend, or perhaps someone with whom you are in conflict reveals in new ways the grace that is ours through God's self-giving love.

The persons who impose ashes do not have to be clergy. It is customary in some large congregations for bowls of ashes to be passed down the pews. The persons carrying the bowls proceed in the same pattern as ushers passing offering plates. They mark the forehead of the first person in each pew, hand the bowl to him/her, and that person turns and marks the next one. As in the plan above, the congregation needs to be reminded of the words and method of imposition before worship begins. In smaller congregations, this method can also be used effectively and is sometimes less intimidating than asking worshipers to come forward.

For many congregations, Ash Wednesday is the most formal and traditional observance of the year. The prayer of confession based on Psalm 51, the Invitation to the Observance of Lenten Discipline, the going forward to kneel in penitence and receive the mark of the cross as a reminder of our baptism, all lead to a vital time of self-examination and preparation. Most recent worship books include the celebration of the Lord's Supper as part of the full Ash Wednesday service. Thus the highly emotional significance of the observance is held together by a liturgy that has varied little over time. In keeping with the formality of the setting, traditional hymns are sung, and a choir or octet may lead Gregorian or Taizé chants for the musical responses.

In any setting, Spirituals are appropriate for congregational singing. "There Is a Balm in Gilead," for example, connects the anointing of God's healing with the mark of the ashes we will receive. Thomas A. Dorsey's "Precious Lord, Take My Hand" works well too, sung or played—I once heard an especially haunting rendition played by a solo saxophone from the balcony of a large church—encouraging those gathering to reflect on the themes of this day. Most resources recommend that if there is a processional, it should be done in silence, but quiet music that is reflective of the occasion may be played before the service begins and during times of meditation. Silence is an important element of worship too, especially after the prayer of confession and the reading of the Scripture.

Another possibility for some communities is the practice of holding ecumenical Ash Wednesday services outdoors as vigils in times of crisis or mourning. One such service was held in March 2003 in Lafayette Square in front of the White House, sponsored by the Roman Catholic group Pax Christi, as a witness for the peace of Christ. In these settings worshipers stand in a circle and join in prayers, readings, and familiar songs; the ashes are passed around the circle as described above.

The observance of Ash Wednesday can strengthen the whole community and remind us of the need for communal reckoning. If God, the lover of justice, sent Christ, who is our peace, to die for the world's suffering, our attention will be drawn on Ash Wednesday, not only to our individual mortality and sinfulness, but to our need to work for God's reign of justice and peace throughout the earth and our interconnectedness with all creation. Reflecting this concern for our neighbors and all that God has created, the Prayers of Intercession are the one variable in the prayers of most traditional services. They may follow a recognizable pattern, as in the example below, but they will resonate with current concerns for individuals, the church, and the world.

Prayers of Intercession for Ash Wednesday

Merciful God,
We are your servants;
we bear on our brow the mark of Jesus who died:
Give us grace to remember our baptism into Jesus' death
and our hope of being raised like him to life like his.
Lord in your mercy,

hear our prayer.

God of all the earth, your whole creation groans in pain,
waiting for redemption:
Guide us to be faithful caretakers of the earth;
Teach us to guard the lives of all your creatures
and protect the air we breathe and the water we drink.
Help us to remember *(name of place)* damaged by flood,
. . . ravaged by storm; . . . destroyed by earthquake;
and lead us to deplore human disregard for precious lands.
Lord in your mercy,

hear our prayer.

God of all the nations,
heal the wounds that we inflict on each other;
break the barriers of race and clan.
Guide governments and rulers to turn swords to plowshares
and seek freedom for the oppressed;
Grant to *(names of nations)* an end to their conflict,
that they may live in peace and their people may return home.
Grant healing to the people of *(name of country)*;
free them from famine and disease.
Grant to our own country and its leaders the will
to seek your justice and remember the needs of your children.
Especially we remember *(names of leaders)*;
guide them in time of crisis.
Lord in your mercy,

hear our prayer.

God, you are the father of all consolation,
the mother of all compassion:
Comfort those who grieve and those who are dying.

Bring your healing touch to the sick
and sustain those in trouble of any kind.
Remember those we name aloud
and those we name in our hearts:
(Names are read)
Lord in your mercy,

hear our prayer.

Mighty God, the love of your Son Jesus abides in us
and your Holy Spirit anoints us to forgive, heal, and baptize in
   his name:
Guide your church to proclaim the gospel in unity
and work for your reign of peace.
Remember our pastors *(names)* and denominational leaders;
give strength to all our members
   and show them their gifts for ministry.
Lead those who work on mission fields and in ecumenical
   agencies,
and support congregations who work with those in need.
Give us a holy Lent and prepare us to observe with devotion
the time of our Lord's passion, death, and resurrection.
Lord in your mercy,

hear our prayer.

God, most gracious and holy,
keep us faithful to your word,
wash us in the river of the water of life,
and help us to walk in newness
that we may join with all your saints
in the song of everlasting joy,
through Jesus Christ our Lord. **Amen.**

Holy Thursday

A few years ago I received a phone call from my nineteen-year-old son, away from home for the first time during Holy Week visiting a college friend whose family was not religiously observant. My son had gone to church all his life until he went away to college, and now he suddenly realized something was missing. In his call to me that Tuesday morning, he said, "Mom, what is it we do on Maundy Thursday? I'm going to church here, even if no one else does." He was not too clear on the details, but he knew from childhood memories working on his imagination: something important will happen in church on this Thursday.

Holy Thursday observances are full of possibilities for preaching and for symbolic actions, focused on the actions of Jesus and his disciples on the night of his betrayal. If all the pieces of this rich tradition are to be included in the service, adequate time and preparation is essential. Worship on Holy Thursday can take place in a remarkable variety of settings, from a formal service in a large sanctuary to a potluck in a fellowship hall, and still retain an integrity and significance that is lasting. The impressive rites have a long-term effect and work on the imagination after more cerebral experiences have faded.

The strangest thing we do, of course, is the foot-washing. Long resisted in many congregations, foot-washing is at the heart of Jesus' commandment, given on this night, to love one another. We are beginning to understand the radical nature of this act: that it echoes the image of Jesus given in the Philippians hymn: "Christ Jesus . . . emptied himself, taking the form of a slave, being born in human likeness. And being found in human form, he humbled himself and became obedient to the point of death—even death on a cross."

Jesus, the household slave, becomes our servant on the night before his passion. Jesus is the slave who becomes our risen Lord.

There is no adequate substitute for foot-washing, but if there is strong resistance, it can be done with a small number of persons—usually twelve—chosen to represent the congregation and prepared ahead of time. The persons chosen should be truly representative in age, gender, ethnic, and vocational diversity. They are called forward and the rite takes place in the chancel area.

In congregations that meet on this night in the fellowship hall, the bowl, towel, and pitcher may be passed among those seated at the table before dinner is served. In this way, those who choose not to participate can do so without seeming too obvious about it.

Even if there is no foot-washing, some recognition of this act will be made in the sermon and prayers. Members of the congregation may also be given an opportunity to commit themselves to acts of charity and love in recognition of the new commandment of Jesus, the *mandatum novum,* from which the designation Maundy Thursday came. One idea is to ask a group in the congregation to organize the collection of new, white towels to be brought to the service and placed on a table by the entrance to the sanctuary. The towels may be worn as stoles by the worship leaders—ushers, acolytes, communion servers, choir, readers, clergy—in recognition of their servant leadership. Following the service, the towels are donated to a homeless shelter or other charity.

The Lord's Supper is the central act of Holy Thursday, and if a meal was served in the fellowship hall, Communion may take place around the tables after everyone has eaten and the dishes have been cleared. Following Communion, the worshipers move to the sanctuary in procession for the Stripping of the Church and Tenebrae or the dismissal, which will take place in as much darkness as safety allows.

The Stripping of the Church is a rite that symbolizes Jesus' humiliation at his crucifixion. If done effectively, it is difficult to watch and yet mesmerizing. The movements should be precise, almost choreographed, and done in silence. Teenagers or older children may be asked to help, and, given proper rehearsal, often perform this task with seriousness of purpose and great dignity. Everything should be removed, including the Bible, and carried in procession out of the sanctuary.

Table Grace for Holy Thursday

God our Shepherd, you provide us with good things:
We thank you for this food and for the friendship at this table.
Help us to be good friends of Jesus
and serve the needy in his name.
Renew us by your Spirit and prepare us for the coming days;
teach us to remember Jesus' death and resurrection in acts of
     love.
In the name of Jesus Christ our Lord. **Amen.**

Where Charity and Love Prevail

God of love,
your Son Jesus on the night he was betrayed,
proclaimed to us a new commandment, love for one another:
Bind us in that love and make us servants of each other.
Let conflict be unknown among us,
and lead us to forgive one another as you forgive us.
Help us to seek you among those who need you most,
to empty ourselves of all envy and pride,
and become joyful servants of the poor and suffering.
Wash us and prepare us to celebrate the obedience of Jesus,
whose love led him to the cross. In his name. **Amen.**

Thanksgiving After Communion

Holy God,
we have feasted in memory of the night Jesus was betrayed
and in the confidence that we will feast again with him in glory:
We give you thanks for the gift of this meal,
     shared among friends.
We give you thanks for the gift of Jesus' life,
     his body broken for us.
Give us grace to feed the hungry
in the name of the One who died and was raised from death,
that the world might have life.
In the name of Jesus Christ our Lord. **Amen.**

Good Friday

On Good Friday the church is united in its reverence and awe before the crucified Jesus. As a sign of our unity, the newer denominational worship books all follow the same basic pattern for Good Friday worship. We enter a bare church, sing the hymns of the cross, pray as a community, engage in silent meditation and spoken reflection, and hear again the story of Jesus' passion with our eyes on the cross. The congregation, large or small, gathers to pray in sorrow for the world's alienation and in thanksgiving for God's self-giving love. No embellishment is necessary, but careful preparation and thought are essential to lift up this holy day with integrity and dignity.

What are the considerations for worship planners? How do we proclaim in quiet simplicity but with unwavering hope what we know of God's unbounded love for the world and what remains the great mystery of our faith? The communal prayers, the reading of the Scripture, and the time of silent prayer and meditation are primary considerations.

Opening Prayer

> God our Savior, you gave us your beloved Son,
>   Israel's strength and consolation, hope of all the earth;
> you abandoned him to the agony of the cross,
>   so that the abandoned people of the world might have life:
> Lift our hearts and bring us together beneath the cross,
>   ready to leave behind our sin and fear,
> confident in the grace that brings us into your abiding love,
>   for you will prevail and death itself will die.
> In the name of the Crucified One, whose victory is life. **Amen.**

Call to Confession

Jesus calls all who are heavily burdened to come to the cross and lay before him all our cares and sorrows. At the cross of Jesus we will find mercy and love.

Prayer of Confession

Merciful God,
we confess to you and to one another,
that we have sinned in thought, word, and deed.
We have neglected your works of justice and mercy;
we have failed to love our neighbors as ourselves;
we have not loved one another as Christ has loved us;
we have not forgiven others as we have been forgiven.

Lord, have mercy.
Christ, have mercy.
Lord, have mercy.

Take us by the hand and lead us to the cross of Jesus;
guide us on the path to peace and life,
for the sake of your Son, who bore our sins in his body. Amen.

Words of Assurance

He left his Father's throne above
(so free, so infinite his grace!),
emptied himself of all but love,
and bled for Adam's helpless race.
'Tis mercy all, immense and free,
for O my God, it found out me!
(Charles Wesley, "And Can It Be," 1739)

By Jesus' wounds we are healed and forgiven.
Thanks be to God.

The Intercessions

Loving God, you sent your Son into the world,
not to condemn the world,

117

but that, through him, the world might be saved:
Hear us as we pray to you
in sorrow for the anguish of our sin
and in hope for the spring of eternal life
that pours from the cross of Christ.

Hear us as we pray for people everywhere,
   according to their need.
Send your Spirit to intercede for us when words fail us.

For the holy church throughout the world,
for its people who love and serve others,
for all who suffer for the sake of Christ,
for those preparing for baptism, confirmation, and new
   ministries,
and for those who work to reconcile us in love:
Strengthen them that they may grow in your grace
and give them the peace of Christ.
Savior God, hear our prayer.

Lord, have mercy.

For the nations of earth and their leaders,
for all who work to end conflict and war;
for our own country, its president, legislators, judges,
civil servants, and women and men in military service:
Rule in the hearts and minds of those in authority
that they may be subject to your justice.
Startle us with your mercy and lead us to peace
that we may proclaim liberty throughout the land.
Savior God, hear our prayer.

Lord, have mercy.

For all who suffer in body and mind,
for victims of violence and abuse,
for those who have lost loved ones and those in despair,
for the sick, the dying, and all who care for them:
Sustain them, help them to know your presence,
and to receive your healing power.
Savior God, hear our prayer.

Lord, have mercy.

For all children, those whose lives are a joy in our midst,
and those whose lives are at risk from famine and disease,
for those who are neglected and those who are homeless,
for children who receive inadequate health care and education:
Teach us to provide for their needs from your abundant gifts.
Restore our sons and daughters,
protect and bring them into your community of love.
Savior God, hear our prayer.

Lord, have mercy.

For the earth and all its creatures,
for the oceans threatened by waste,
for the forests injured by carelessness,
for the air and water that once were pure,
for the crowded habitats of all living things:
Give us grace to care for all that you have made
and live in harmony with creation that all may have life.
Savior God, hear our prayer.

Lord, have mercy.

For all prisoners and those on trial,
for those who live in fear of violence,
and those who are victims of unjust practices,
for all persons who are condemned to die:
Hear their cries and share their grief;
Redeem them by your mercy;
draw them nearer to the cross of Jesus.
Savior God, hear our prayer.

Lord, have mercy.

For all who seek to live by God's truth,
for ourselves, our neighbors, our loved ones, our enemies:
Help us to cast on you our grief and anxiety;
guide us through the valley of the shadow of death.
Turn our faces upward toward the cross.
Savior God, hear our prayer.

Lord, have mercy.

In the name of the One who poured out himself to death,
your Son, our Savior, Jesus Christ. **Amen.**

The Reading of the Scripture

Isaiah 52:13–53:12

The first reading deserves great care in its proclamation. The early church struggled to understand the cross in conversation with the Hebrew prophets, and Isaiah's servant songs, in particular, shaped their thinking. The Isaiah reading for Good Friday, though moving, is long and poetically complex. To make it more accessible to the ear, it can be divided as below for two voices or a lead voice and a choir of readers. In either case careful rehearsal is required, and in no case should the reading be allowed to drag because of overly slow or ponderous intonation.

The Fourth Servant Song

See, my servant shall prosper;
  he shall be exalted and lifted up,
  and shall be very high. . . .
So he shall startle many nations:
  kings shall shut their mouths because of him;
for that which had not been told them they shall see,
  and that which they had not heard they shall contemplate.

Who has believed what we have heard?
  And to whom has the arm of the LORD been revealed? . . .
He had no form or majesty that we should look at him,
  nothing in his appearance that we should desire him.
He was despised and rejected by others;
  a man of suffering and acquainted with infirmity. . . .

Surely he has borne our infirmities
  and carried our diseases;
yet we accounted him stricken,
  struck down by God, and afflicted.
But he was wounded for our transgressions,
  crushed for our iniquities;
upon him was the punishment that made us whole,
  and by his bruises we are healed.

All we like sheep have gone astray;

we have all turned to our own way,
and the LORD has laid on him the iniquity of us all.

He was oppressed, and he was afflicted,
 yet he did not open his mouth;
like a lamb that is led to the slaughter,
 and like a sheep that before its shearers is silent,
 so he did not open his mouth.

By a perversion of justice he was taken away.
 Who could have imagined his future?
For he was cut off from the land of the living,
 stricken for the transgression of my people.

They made his grave with the wicked
 and his tomb with the rich;
although he had done no violence,
 and there was no deceit in his mouth.

Yet it was the will of the LORD to crush him with pain.
When you make his life an offering for sin,
 he shall see his offspring, and shall prolong his days;
 through him the will of the LORD shall prosper.

Out of his anguish he shall see light;
 he shall find satisfaction through his knowledge.
The righteous one, my servant, shall make many righteous,
 and he shall bear their iniquities.

Therefore I will allot him a portion with the great,
 and he shall divide the spoil with the strong;
 because he poured out himself to death,
 and was numbered with the transgressors;
yet he bore the sin of many,
 and made intercession for the transgressors.

Psalm 22

The Psalm is read or sung by the congregation from the psalter. The psalms in *The United Methodist Hymnal* (p. 752) and *The New Century Hymnal* (p. 632), for example, are pointed for singing or chanting with a sung response. *The Presbyterian Hymnal* (# 168) has a versified version of Psalm 22 set to Sarum plainsong.

Hebrews 10:16-25

The epistle should be read pastorally. Its assurance—we have been "sprinkled clean" and "washed with pure water"—is what gives us the courage to approach the cross in prayer. On this night we are to remember our baptism and be thankful. The emphasis here is also on community: we are to encourage one another and "provoke one another to love and good deeds" (vv. 24-25). Alone we cannot face the enormity of what Jesus suffered for us on the cross, but Jesus lifted on the cross draws us all together in communion with God. If the congregation is small, ask them to form a circle, joining hands, for this reading and a brief prayer following it, illuminating the uniting power of the cross for the community of faith. The reading may also be followed by a hymn.

John 18:1–19:42

The presentation of the passion narrative as a dramatic reading gives it embodiment and takes it out of the usual way we do things. There are problems, however, if the readers approach John's account as a play to be performed. The amount of time and work—memorization, character development, and rehearsal—necessary to perform it effectively is an unrealistic expectation in most situations. And turning the Gospel reading into a performance is problematic on many levels.

Another caution concerning the integrity of the presentation is to remember that it is a Scripture reading, and adding to the text of John's Gospel in an attempt to add details of the story from the other Gospels is not a good practice. One reason for hearing the passion story twice each year—read from Matthew, Mark, or Luke on Palm/Passion Sunday and John on Good Friday—is that we need a variety of witnesses; we need to hear both an account from the Synoptics and John's subtly nuanced narration. Attempting to present a reading that is a mixture of all four Gospels obliterates the unique perspective of each witness and narrows our understanding.

One problem with John's text, however, is his use of the term "the Jews." It is clear throughout John's Gospel that the author means by "the Jews" not the Jewish people but a relatively small group of Jewish leaders who opposed Jesus. Any observance of Good Friday must be framed in the awareness of the potential for unthinkable harm—and the horror that has already been propagated—as a result of blaming "the Jews" for the crucifixion. Careful interpretation of John's terminology, recognition of Rome's responsibility for the crucifixion, and an understanding of the role our own sin plays in Jesus' sacrifice is essential. Some biblical scholars have suggested the substitution of the words "religious authorities" for "the Jews" in reading the Gospel at public worship. This substitution shifts our focus to the way some "religious authorities," even some modern Christians, have always guarded their power and are closed to the new thing God is doing.

Proclaiming John's Passion Narrative in Procession

One way to add movement and drama that is in keeping with liturgical tradition is to have the reading of the passion narrative done in procession. When the time comes for the Gospel reading, the readers enter through the main door led by a cross-bearer, two candle-bearers with large, lighted candles, and a Bible-bearer carrying an open Bible. The readers include a narrator, a reader to speak Jesus' words, and two or three other readers who will divide the remaining parts among them. In John's account only the temple authorities and police cry, "Crucify him," so a small group of people can read this part in procession with the others or from the choir loft.

All readers will have scripts, printed in large type, with their parts well marked. The text can be downloaded from a number of Bible web sites and printed out with appropriate directions added and dialogue separated from narration. An example of how this is done is found on pages 180-86 of *The New Handbook of the Christian Year* (Hoyt L. Hickman et al., Nashville: Abingdon Press, 1992). The New Revised Standard Version is the preferred translation for reading in worship, but if another translation is used, choose one that is well received for its accuracy of translation as well as contemporary language and readability. Place the scripts in black folders for carrying.

Below are suggestions for dividing the text into five sections and reading each from a different location in the worship space. The locations, of course, must be chosen with specific logistics and acoustics in mind. In smaller churches no amplification should be necessary, but in a large space a good sound system with cordless microphones is essential. In all cases readers should rehearse in the space and practice projection techniques.

- The readers, candle-bearers, and Bible-bearer enter the main door led by the cross-bearer.
- The procession stops halfway down the center aisle, and John 18:1-18 is read.
- The procession moves all the way down the aisle and proceeds to the right of center, faces the congregation, and John 18:19-27 is read. The narrator may read the transition sentence as they move.
- The procession moves to the left of center, faces the congregation, and John 18:28-38*a* is read.
- The procession moves back to the center, still on the lower level, and John 18:38*b*–19:16*a* is read.
- The procession moves up to the center of the cancel area. The narrator at this point may read from the lectern. The others group themselves appropriately with the reader who speaks the words of Jesus at the center. The cross-bearer stands to this reader's side and slightly behind him/her. The Bible will remain in the hands of the bearer to be carried out with the candles at the end of the reading, leaving the church bear again, except for the cross. John 19:16*b*-42 is read.
- When the reading is finished, the readers remain in place while the cross is placed in its stand at the center in front of or behind the communion table where it remains during the time of meditation.
- The readers, led by the bearers, exit in silence.

A hymn or solo may follow the Gospel reading. *Suggestion:* "Were You There When They Crucified My Lord?"

Meditation Before the Cross

Many books of worship include the Reproaches of the Cross as a structure for meditation on Good Friday, reviving an ancient tradition. The newer versions rely on the work of the Inter-Lutheran Commission on Worship, which has provided an admirable recasting of the Reproaches in contemporary language and eliminated all references that could be construed as anti-Jewish in sentiment. Verse 9 of the Reproaches makes clear, in fact, that the church is guilty of making God's beloved covenant people of Israel "scapegoats for your own guilt."* The Reproaches thus become a reminder to us of the horrific devastation that Christians have allowed or propagated against the Jewish people in the name of revenge for the crucifixion.

An alternative to the Reproaches is to encourage silent prayer and meditation before the cross. During the singing of a hymn, such as "When I Survey the Wondrous Cross," worshipers are invited to move forward toward the cross. The cross that was carried in procession should occupy a central location and be the visual focus that invites worshipers to pray and reflect silently. Those who can kneel should do so, but others may be encouraged to sit in the front pews or to stand to one side or the other.

It is sometimes helpful to provide guidance or direction for prayer. The planning committee, for example, can print cards that list phrases from Scripture for meditation and appropriate intercessions for this day (see pp. 126-27). These can be distributed with the bulletin or placed on a small table at a convenient place. The prayer cards can also be taken by parish visitors to the sick and others unable to attend the Good Friday observance.

There is no dismissal or closing music on Good Friday in recognition of the fact that this act of worship is not complete until the announcement of the resurrection on Easter. Worshipers are encouraged to pray before the cross for as long as they wish. An announcement to this effect should be placed in the bulletin so that worshipers know not to expect words of dismissal.

---

* Hoyt L. Hickman, Don E. Saliers, Laurence Hull Stookey, James F. White, *The New Handbook of the Christian Year* (Nashville: Abingdon Press, 1992), 189.

SCRIPTURE FOR MEDITATION

All we like sheep have gone astray;
    we have all turned to our own way,
and the LORD has laid on him the iniquity of us all. . . .
By a perversion of justice he was taken away.
Out of his anguish he shall see light. . . .
He poured out himself to death,
    and was numbered with the transgressors.

(Isaiah 53:6 ,8a,11a, 12b)

So they took Jesus, and carrying the cross by
himself, he went out to what is called The Place of the
Skull, which in Hebrew is called Golgotha.
There they crucified him. . . .
When Jesus had received the wine, he said, "It is finished."
Then he bowed his head and gave up his spirit.

(John 19:16b–18a; 30)

"And I, when I am lifted up from the earth, will draw all
people to myself."

(John 12:32)

For the message of the cross is foolishness to those who
are perishing, but to us who are being saved it is the
power of God.

(1 Corinthians 1:18)

You know that you were ransomed . . . with the precious
blood of Christ, like that of a lamb without defect or
blemish. . . .
Through him you have come to trust in God, who raised
him from the dead.

(1 Peter 1:18a, 19, 21)

NRSV

INTERCESSIONS FOR SILENT PRAYER

God, in your great mercy you have sent your Son to save the world from death. In remembrance of his suffering, let us pray

for the earth and all that God has created.

for the church in every land and for our own congregation, its pastors, lay leaders, and all its members.

for the peoples of the world, for governments and leaders, for peace and justice.

for the sick and the dying, for those who mourn, for those in distress.

for our friends and family that they may have your guidance, that they may have health and hear your words of encouragement.

for ourselves, that we may lead faithful lives, giving thanks for our baptism into Jesus' death and our rising with Jesus into new life.

In the name of Jesus, our Savior.
Amen.

The Easter Vigil

The people gather in silence and in near darkness. It's eleven o'clock at night; we have traveled to the middle of nowhere; yet we know we belong here, waiting in great expectation. St. John's Benedictine Abbey, in sparsely populated Minnesota farm country, is seventy miles northwest of the Twin Cities, and there are still patches of spring snow on the Abbey grounds. In spite of the remote location, fifteen hundred worshipers fill the Abbey Church for the Great Vigil of Easter. The church building itself was clearly designed for this celebration. A vast, modern stone structure, it has been stripped bare of banners and paraments on Thursday, and as we sit in the gloomy half-light, it puts us in mind of a tomb. The only visible light is one shaft from the square lantern high above us.

The silence is finally broken as we hear rustling in the corridor at our right. Through the clear windows we can barely make out the shadowy figures of two hundred monks proceeding from the cloister. As they approach, the vigil fire burns in the brazier near the large baptismal pool at the entrance of the church. The paschal candle is lighted from the fire, and the Service of Light begins.

"The light of Christ rises in glory, overcoming the darkness of sin and death."

"Light of Christ! Thanks be to God"

The monks' candles are lighted from the paschal candle, and that light is passed to all the worshipers, who also hold candles. The paschal candle is carried through the church and the sung acclamation "Light of Christ! Thanks be to God" is repeated. Finally almost two thousand candles fill the church with light. Following the singing of the Easter proclamation, the Exsultet, individual candles are extinguished, bright lights come on, and the Service of the Word begins.

Now we are swept along on a journey through the Scriptures that takes our breath away by its scope and beauty. The excellent readers and musicians represent the community: brothers and priests, staff members, professors and students at St. John's University and St. Benedict's College, and nuns from St. Benedict's convent. Seven Old Testament lessons are read, each followed by a biblical canticle and sung response. The epistle reading is Romans 6:3-11, which likens our baptism to "dying and rising with Christ." Then comes the resurrection narrative, which is sung from one of the Synoptic Gospels— Mark, the year I was in attendance. The singing of the Gospel is preceded and followed by a jubilant chorus of "Alleluias," which, with perfect timing, occurs as the Abbey bells are ringing midnight. The abbot preaches a fine and very brief homily following the Gospel.

The Service of Water is next, and in parishes candidates who have prepared for this night will be baptized. This service also includes the reaffirmation of baptismal vows by the entire assembly and sprinkling with generous amounts of water spread joyfully to the farthest corners of the church. The Service of the Bread and Cup completes the Vigil, and when we finally dare to look at our watches, it is 1:30 A.M. No one, not even our twelve-year-old, complains about the length of the service, and, half an hour later, we are surrounded by the community in the Great Hall, laughing, sharing Easter greetings, and enjoying fresh baked hot-cross buns and orange juice.

This celebration, with its origins in the early centuries of Christianity, has been brought back to us in recent years through ecumenical dialogue and the publication of new denominational worship books. Many congregations, however, find the idea of holding a Vigil service that begins late on Holy Saturday evening intimidating and not even practical, especially in places where Easter sunrise services are well-established traditions. There are nevertheless several good reasons to consider celebrating an Easter Vigil, including the obvious one of the opportunity to worship at Easter as our ancestors in the faith did.

First, it is important to understand that the legacy of the Vigil is not limited to churches with high liturgical traditions. The Vigil is four services in one, and by far the longest and most dramatic is the Service of the Word. For those of us who are steeped in the word of God, who call ourselves "people of the word," this journey through six or more key Scriptures on our way to acclaiming God's great plan for salvation that began at the creation is the highlight of the year.

Also the Vigil helps make clear that the worship that begins on Holy Thursday is not complete until the Easter proclamation of the resurrection is made. Jesus' death and resurrection belong together and cannot be easily divided into separate observances for the convenience of modern schedules. In some traditions the prayers and other acts of worship are continuous from sunset on Thursday until sunset on Easter Day; this time is known as the Triduum or Great Three Days. Not all worshipers remain the entire three days, but someone is keeping watch, and everyone comes back at some point on each day, including Saturday. The Saturday between Good Friday and Easter Day in our culture is too often treated like any other day, as if it meant nothing but a brief break in the crowded Holy Week schedule. Traditionally it has been kept as a day of fasting, prayer, and anticipation, which can only end in the dark hour of midnight when the Easter Alleluias break through.

A more implicit consideration is that we sometimes neglect at Easter our most faithful congregants. The full morning services of Easter Day are a joy to behold, but packed parking lots and standing-room-only crowds making their once-a-year appearance are off-putting to some regular worshipers. And in denominations that have "Communion Sunday" once a month, there is rarely a Eucharistic service on Easter Day, the day when all facets of this sacrament rise to our consciousness. For the faithful members who will welcome a chance to proclaim Easter late on Saturday evening, the Vigil offers Easter communion at its close, and an opportunity throughout the evening to minister to each other, including the congregation's ministering to the pastor through Scripture reading and song.

Here are some ideas for including the Easter Vigil in your Easter celebrations.

1. With a group of church members who want to encourage a deeper celebration of Easter in your congregation, visit a fully celebrated Easter Vigil in a large Roman Catholic, Lutheran, or

Episcopal church. Visit an abbey church or an Episcopal Cathedral. If there is not one in your town, ask a delegation to make attending one part of a spring trip. Washington's National Cathedral, for example, is a welcoming place for ecumenical visitors. Call the Cathedral ahead for information about time; in some places it will be necessary to arrive early in order to get a good seat. Those who will attend may study the traditions of the Vigil ahead of time and, when they return, make a report to the worship commission or church council.

2. If your congregation has a sunrise service tradition, consider beginning just before dawn, in the darkness, and using the liturgy in your worship book for the Easter Vigil, starting with the lighting of the paschal candle from the Vigil fire. If the liturgy is used in the early morning hours, it is called "The First Service of Easter." Following communion, breakfast can be served before the regular Easter Sunday morning schedule begins.

3. Many large congregations have a regular Saturday evening service that some worshipers prefer to attend in place of Sunday morning. When it comes to Easter, there is a problem. Can we with integrity have a service at six o'clock Saturday evening that is a duplicate of the one to come on Easter Sunday morning? Consider on this special night starting the Saturday service somewhat later—anytime after dark—and using the Vigil liturgy. Prepare the congregation by introducing the Vigil in newsletters, commission meetings, and Sunday school classes. Encourage regular worshipers to attend both on Saturday evening and Sunday morning. This will serve the dual purpose of offering a full Easter liturgy—the ancient tradition and symbolism of the Vigil and the festivity of Sunday morning—and allow worshipers who don't usually come at the same time to be together, something that is all too rare in big churches. Follow the Vigil service with a time of food and fellowship.

4. Don't be afraid to start with small numbers. At Metropolitan Memorial United Methodist Church in Washington, D.C., the Vigil celebration was begun in the early 1990s and at first was attended by only a fraction of its twelve-hundred members. A vigil fire blazed on the church porch, and the small but highly involved congregation processed from there, led by the paschal candle, to the choir of the Gothic-style church where the worshipers sat. The Scriptures were read from a lectern placed on the level below them. The readers were members of a well-rehearsed chancel drama group, with varied cadences and timbres that enlivened the readings. The sung responses were stanzas or choruses of familiar hymns that everyone could sing. The senior pastor and the music director were relieved of all duties in light of their obligations the next morning, allowing a maximum of lay participation in leadership roles. Those who attended enjoyed the small group atmosphere and the liveliness of the ages-old liturgy.

5. In small congregations, it may be that everyone who attends will have a reading, a musical response, or a prayer to offer. The music may be congregational singing, using the hymnal. Having everyone participate as a leader in some part of the Vigil is well worth the effort it takes to coordinate. The pastor or worship leader will have as a primary responsibility seeing that the symbolic acts involving fire, light, water, word, bread and cup are done with care and integrity.

6. Think of the special needs of your congregation at Easter. One example is planning an appropriate celebration for the confirmation of those who have been preparing for full membership. Congregations who have confirmation services at Easter are searching for times other than Palm Sunday or Easter Day, already full and lengthy celebrations that may not allow the amount of time due this important rite for young people and their families. Brentwood United Methodist Church near Nashville, Tennessee, a congregation of more than five-thousand members, has its confirmation service at the Easter Vigil on Saturday evening. Brentwood regularly has confirmation classes of more than 100 youth, some of whom have not been baptized as infants. Baptizing, reaffirming baptismal vows, and confirming are appropriately done during the Vigil's Service of the Water.

7. In preparation for the Vigil night, plan Lenten study sessions that introduce the Scripture readings of the Easter Vigil. These sessions may be for adult classes on Sunday morning or small group sessions held midweek during lent. A brief outline of possible sessions follows.

A Lenten Study of the Easter Vigil Scripture Readings

Week of Lent 1

Introduce the Easter Vigil, referring to its ancient roots and its worldwide and ecumenical usage.

Explain what a canticle or biblical song is, giving examples from Psalms, Isaiah, and Luke. Show how these songs may be used as responses to other readings in worship.

Discuss the purpose of having a wide variety of readings for Easter worship, pointing out that the God of Israel, creator and deliverer, the God of the covenant, is the same God who raised Jesus from the dead.

Define and discuss the terms "saving events" and "salvation history."

Read Genesis 1:1–2:2 and Psalm 33.
How do we worship God as creator? How does God's work of creation continue? What do we mean by "God's new creation in Christ"? Find and sing a hymn that reflects this reading.

Write a collect* based on this week's Scriptures.

Week of Lent 2

Read Genesis 7:1-5, 11-18; 8:6-18; 9:8-13 and Psalm 46.
What covenant did God make with Noah? With the earth? How does God's plan for salvation include God's intention to redeem the earth (see also Romans 8:18-25)? Find and sing a hymn that reflects this reading.

Read Genesis 22:1-18 and Psalm 16.
What does this story tell us about God's covenant with Abraham? About God's covenant with us? Why do you think this reading is included in the Easter Vigil? Find and sing a hymn that reflects this reading.

Write a collect* based on this week's Scriptures.

Week of Lent 3

Read Exodus 14:10–15:1 and Exodus 15:1-6, 11-13, 17-21.
This reading contains one of the oldest portions of the Bible—Miriam's song, Exodus 15:20-21—and it is never left out of the Vigil readings. Why do you think it is important to remember this story at Easter? The name for Easter in early Christianity was the Paschal (Passover) Feast. Why is Easter called the Christian Passover? How do we worship God as deliverer? What does it mean to be delivered from slavery to sin and death? Find and sing a hymn that reflects this reading.

Write a collect* based on this week's Scriptures.

Week of Lent 4

Read Isaiah 54:5-14 and Psalm 30.
What does it mean that the Lord has compassion on us? What is God's covenant of peace? How do we ensure that our children—all children—are taught by the Lord? What does verse 14 say to our situation today? Find and sing a hymn that reflects this reading.

Read Isaiah 55:1-11 and Isaiah 12:2-6.
In Isaiah 55, what invitation is issued in verse 1? What does Isaiah 55 tell us about the heavenly banquet? What does God's offer of food and drink without price mean for us today? What does verse 3 say to us at Easter? Who is God calling in verse 5? How do verses 6-9 speak to our observance of Lent? How was God's purpose accomplished in Jesus? Find and sing a hymn that reflects this reading.

Write a collect* based on this week's Scriptures.

Week of Lent 5

Read Ezekiel 37:1-14 and Psalm 143.
What does God's spirit do in this reading? How are God's spirit and God's breath related? Compare this story to Jesus' visit to the disciples after the resurrection in John 20:19-23. Why do we include Pentecost in our celebration of Easter? How do we wor-

ship God as life-giver? Find and sing a hymn that reflects this reading.

Read Zephaniah 3:14-20.
Compare this reading with Zechariah 9:9-11 and Jesus' Palm Sunday entry into Jerusalem. What does it mean for God to rejoice over us (Zephaniah 3:17)? How do we worship God as victor? How is Jesus a victor on the cross? Find and sing a hymn that reflects this reading.

Write a collect* based on this week's Scriptures.

Holy Week
Read Romans 6:3-11 and Psalm 114.
What do we learn from this reading about baptism? What do we learn about Jesus' death and resurrection? What "new thing" does God do in Jesus Christ? How can we prepare to celebrate Easter? Find and sing a hymn that reflects this reading.

Write a collect* based on this week's Scriptures.

*The Collect

The collect is an ancient pattern of prayer that can serve as a model for other prayers. It is short, yet it has a rich content based on biblical texts. Collects attributed to Origen are among the earliest examples of prayers written for the church, and many of Thomas Cranmer's amazing collects still grace the pages of various versions of the *Book of Common Prayer,* both English and American. Collects are usually based on the Scripture for the day and therefore begin with a statement about who God is and what God has already done for us. This assurance emboldens us to add petitions that pray for God's intervention in our present situation. Longer prayers can begin with a collect or several collects that lead into additional petitions and thanksgiving.

In the Easter Vigil, a collect follows each Scripture reading and reflects the content of that reading. Learning about collects and practicing writing them is a fine Lenten discipline. The collects written during the Lenten study sessions may be used with the appropriate Scripture during your congregation's celebration of the Easter Vigil.

The collect usually has five elements: *(1) Address to God; (2) God's attributes or acts on which this prayer is based; (3) The petition; (4) Intended result of the petition; (5) Final doxology.*

Here is a sample collect based on Exodus 14:10–15:1.

Mighty God,	*(1)*
you delivered your people Israel from slavery in Egypt	*(2)*
and set them on the road to the promised land:	
Give us courage to stand firm	*(3)*
and look for your deliverance;	
free us from our fear of sin and death,	
that we may live this day in gladness,	*(4)*
serving you and rejoicing in your love.	
Through Jesus Christ, our Savior	
to whom be honor and glory. **Amen.**	*(5)*

Ascension of the Lord

The Ascension of the Lord is an ancient feast still celebrated in Christian churches around the world, and it has a place in the Easter celebration of all congregations. When we say the Apostles' Creed, we proclaim our belief in the ascension in the same breath as we proclaim that Jesus died and was raised again from the dead: "On the third day he rose again; he ascended into heaven, is seated at the right hand of the Father, and will come again to judge the living and the dead." We are celebrating saving events that proclaim God's power for life and God's willingness to intervene in astounding ways on behalf of the world God created and loves and will not abandon. The Ascension of the Lord is a significant part of the Easter story and another testimony to God's resurrection power.

When Jesus finds Mary Magdalene weeping at the tomb on Easter Day, he calls her name and gently assures her that he is about to ascend to God: "Do not hold on to me, because I have not yet ascended to the Father. But go to my brothers and say to them, 'I am ascending to my Father and your Father, to my God and your God'" (John 20:17). The ascension is thus a cause for rejoicing. Jesus tells the disciples that he is returning to God's right hand to prepare a place for them and sending them the Spirit who will give them power to do mighty works in his name (John 14:28).

In John's Gospel the ascension completes the sequence of descending/ascending Jesus revealed to Nicodemus in John 3:13-15: "No one has ascended into heaven except the one who descended from heaven, the Son of Man. And just as Moses lifted up the serpent in the wilderness, so must the Son of Man be lifted up, that whoever believes in him may have eternal life." The ascension is the culmination of the act of Jesus being lifted up: on the cross, from the grave, and to God's right hand. This is the exaltation of Philippians 2:9: "Therefore God also highly exalted him, and gave him the name that is above every name." Jesus' lifting up points to God's lifting up of all creation. The ascension has to do with us because Jesus is the promise of eternal life, a new heaven and a new earth, God's restoration of creation, God's victory over death.

We can be imaginative with the planning of an Ascension celebration and with the scheduling. There are several possible times if a service on Thursday seems impractical. Early worship traditions include many instances of liturgies taking place on the eve of a feast day. We still worship on Christmas Eve, often in place of Christmas Day, but Pentecost Eve and Easter Eve or Vigil were also significant times of celebration through the centuries and still are in many places. A Wednesday evening service on the Eve of Ascension Day offers a chance to revive this tradition and worship at a time when some congregations have a regular worship event already scheduled.

Another possibility is to have a church picnic on the following Saturday or Sunday afternoon and close with Ascension of the Lord worship. Holding this celebration out of doors is appropriate for a variety of reasons. Most notably, the ascension is evidence of God's promise to redeem the earth, and therefore, our commitment to caring for creation will be a focus. The date sometimes falls near Earth Day, and connections can be made to that observance through prayers for the earth's well-being. The planning committee may consider planting a tree or flowers on the church grounds as part of the day's activities.

This may be a good occasion to plan an event with a neighboring congregation or to host a group of children or adults who have been part of an outreach program of the congregation. The celebration can also include recognition of new members and their families (see "Acts of Praise," for the Second Sunday of Easter, p. 65). The setting should be festive, whether a picnic area in a park, the church grounds, or fellowship hall. Decorate with balloons and banners, streamers and kites, children's art, and flowers. Ask an experienced game leader to engage as many as are willing in various games; some, at least, should be noncompetitive games and suitable for all ages. Include singing and good food to share in abundance. Bell ringing is an Ascension Day tradition, so ask everyone to bring bells from home to ring at appropriate moments.

The following order of worship is a suggestion for closing the festivities. It is also appropriate for an Ascension Day or Eve service in various settings, including student gatherings, ecumenical meetings, and worship at hospitals or nursing centers.

Ascension of the Lord

The Ringing of the Bells   *(The bells may peal from the church steeple, a bell choir may play, or there may be a joyful cacophony from all the people ringing their own bells.)*

Greeting

> God has called us to the riches of a glorious inheritance among the saints: the immeasurable greatness of God's power for us who believe. God put this power to work in Christ, raised him from the dead, seated him at the right hand of God, and made him the head over all things for the church, which is his body, the fullness of him who fills all in all. Thanks be to God. Alleluia!   *(Based on Ephesians 1:18-20, 22-23)*

Call to Worship

> *(The Leader claps three times before the first line and after the last line; the people respond with three claps.)*
>
> Clap your hand, all peoples!
>
> **Shout to God with loud songs of joy!**
>
> For the Lord, the most high is awesome,
>   a great Ruler over all the earth.
>
> **Sing praises to God, sing praises!**

God has gone up with a shout,
the Lord with the sound of a trumpet.

Sing praises to God, sing praises! *(Psalm 47:1-2, 5-6, paraphrased)*

(Bells may ring.)

Hymn Suggestions: ***"Lord, We Lift Your Name on High,"***
"Crown Him with Many Crowns"

(Bells may ring.)

Opening Prayer

God of glory, Jesus Christ, whom you raised from the dead,
you also raised to reign with you in heavenly places:
Give us grace to stand firm while you clothe us with power from
on high.
Teach us not to look for Jesus in the clouds
but among the little ones, the suffering, and the needy.
Guide us to serve all your people with joy
and to care for the earth that Jesus loves.
In the name of Jesus Christ. **Amen.**

Psalm 121 (Author's paraphrase)

I lift up my eyes to the hills—from where will my help come?

My help comes from the Lord, who made heaven and earth.

He will not let your foot be moved;
the One who keeps you will not slumber.

He who keeps Israel will neither slumber nor sleep.

The Lord is your keeper;
the Lord is your shade at your right hand.

The sun shall not strike you by day, nor the moon by night.

The Lord will keep you from all evil; He will keep your life.

**The Lord will keep your going out and your coming in
from this time on and forevermore.**

Hymn Suggestions: **"For the Beauty of the Earth," "This Is My Father's World"**

Scripture Reading   **Acts 1:1-11 or Luke 24:44-53**

Sermon or Guided Meditation (see suggestions on page 142)

The Apostles' Creed

Hymn   **"Hail the Day That Sees Him Rise"** *(If hymnals are not available, this hymn may be sung as a solo.)*

Prayers of Thanksgiving and Intercession

God our Creator and Redeemer,
you sent your Son Jesus to live with us
and die on the cross to save the whole world.
This same Jesus, you raised from the dead
and brought again on high:
We thank you that Jesus has gone to you
and sends us the Holy Spirit.
We remember with thanksgiving
our baptism into Jesus' death and resurrection.
We give you thanks for the power of your love
that heals and frees us.
We are grateful for your church,
filled with the fullness of Jesus Christ.

Let all the people say:
Thanks be to God. Alleluia!

Thanks be to God. Alleluia!

We thank you, O God, for the beauty of the earth,
for showers of blessing and the sunshine of your joy,
for the shade of trees and the smell of growing things,
for the comfort of dogs and cats who love us,
for the cattle and sheep, secure on the hillside,
for noble beasts, at risk in forests and deserts.
Teach us to protect all your creatures and their homes.
Help us to keep the earth safe and pleasing
for ourselves and generations yet unborn.

Let all the people say:
God, in your goodness, hear our prayer.

God, in your goodness, hear our prayer.

We are mindful, O God, of the needs of your people;
Comfort the sick, the lonely, and those who are sad.
Guide those who are preparing for exams and new jobs.
Protect those who risk their lives to protect others.
Help all travelers and strangers; lead us to welcome them.
Care for the needy and the homeless; give us generous hearts.
Send your grace to all children and those who care for them.
Give health to all people; bless us with long and joyful lives.
Take us at last to the home you have prepared for us
where you reign with Jesus Christ and the Holy Spirit,
  one God now and forever.

Let all the people say:
God, in your goodness, hear our prayer.

God, in your goodness, hear our prayer.

In the name of Jesus Christ, ascended and glorified. **Amen.**

Hymn Suggestion: **"Jesus Shall Reign Where'er the Sun"**

Dismissal and Blessing

See! he lifts his hands above, Alleluia!
See! he shows the prints of love, Alleluia!
Hark! his gracious lips bestow, Alleluia!
Blessings on his church below, Alleluia!
  (Charles Wesley, "Hail the Day That Sees Him Rise")

Go in peace, and may your faith in the Lord Jesus and your
love toward all the saints make you strong. Amen.

(Bells may ring.)

Suggestions for Guided Meditation

Leader:

Today we will reflect together about Jesus and what happened when he left his disciples to return to the right hand of God. On this holy day, called the Ascension of the Lord, we celebrate God's lifting up of Jesus to his rightful place of honor after he had finished the work God sent him to do. This event happened, according to Luke's Gospel, some days after Jesus' resurrection. Jesus came to his disciples, and while they were talking he took them out of the city. As they were watching, he was lifted up and taken away from them. This was an astonishing sight, but Jesus had prepared them, and they knew why he was going. I am going to read some verses from Luke, and then ask you to think about them with me. I will suggest an idea and then pause for silence, giving every one a few moments to think about the significance of what Jesus said and did.

The leader reads Luke 24:49-51 and says:

The last thing the disciples see Jesus do is lift his hands like this *(lift hands)* and bless them. What is a blessing? *(Silence. If answers are given out loud, acknowledge them.)*

We remember Jesus blessing food, when he fed the five thousand *(pause briefly for silent reflection)*; at the supper with the disciples on the night before he was betrayed *(pause)*; on Easter Day at the home of the disciples from Emmaus *(pause)*; when he fed the disciples breakfast on the beach *(pause)*.

We know that Jesus blessed the children, taking them in his arms and placing his hands on their heads *(pause)*. Part of Jesus' blessing was a warning that no one should harm his little ones *(pause)*.

We know that Jesus blesses the earth and all its creatures: the oceans, the trees, the hills, the wild beasts, the cattle, and all our pets *(pause)*. Jesus reminded us that God knows when a tiny sparrow falls to the earth *(pause)*. Jesus came to save the whole world, and he hears the cries of the earth *(pause)*.

We know that Jesus blesses us now as he blessed his disciples *(pause)*. Jesus blesses strangers *(pause)*. Jesus blesses the nations *(pause)*. Jesus blesses the church, not just the building but the people all over the world who love Jesus *(pause)*. Jesus blesses you and me *(pause)*.

When Jesus left his disciples, they were sad. But Jesus told them to be happy, to pray and sing glad songs. Jesus was going to be with God, his Father, where he would make a place ready for us. Jesus also promised to send us a gift, the gift of God's Spirit to comfort and help us. Jesus told us to wait and pray, and we will be clothed with power from on high. Let us pray silently that God's Holy Spirit will fill our lives *(pause)*.

Let us close this time of reflection by saying together John 3:16.

For God so loved the world that he gave his only Son,
so that everyone who believes in him
may not perish but may have eternal life. Alleluia!

PART FOUR

Extending the
Celebration

Household Prayer for Lent

The following order for household prayer is for use from Ash Wednesday through Holy Saturday. It may be copied and distributed, along with the chart of daily scripture readings for Lent, for use in parish households. Each day new scripture readings are added to the order, using the chart of daily readings for Lent on pages 149-150. The second reading may also be a meditation chosen from a Lenten devotional book. Lent is a good time to learn new hymns and teach hymns to children, so sing a hymn if at all possible. Otherwise read a hymn together, choosing one from the index of your hymnal under "Lent."

Prepare a worship center for daily prayer in the household. Cover a small table with a purple or white cloth. Children can help make the cloth by fringing a square of fabric. Choose objects to place on the table that remind you of the season of Lent and invite you to pray together, for example: an open Bible, bare branches, a large white candle, a bowl of water and seashells as reminders of baptism. The candle may be decorated by sticking whole cloves into it in the shape of a cross.

Call to Prayer

> *Leader:* Create in us clean hearts, O God,
> and renew in us the spirit of our baptism.

> *People:* **God's word is near to us, on our lips and in our heart.**
> **Thanks be to God. Amen.**

Lighting of the Candle

> *Leader:* Once we lived in the shadows,
> but now in God we are light.
> May God help us to live as children of light,
> enjoying all that is good and right and true,
> and doing what is pleasing to the Lord.
> *(Based on Ephesians 5:8-10)*

Hymn Suggestions: **"Fairest Lord Jesus," "Jesus Loves Me"**

Scripture Reading
(from daily readings)

Second Reading
(a second daily Scripture reading, a psalm, or a devotional meditation)

Prayers

> *Leader:* In the quiet of this holy time of Lent let us pray together. *(Silent prayers)*
>
> *Spoken prayers: Anyone can speak short prayers of petition and thanksgiving.*
>
> *The leader prays this or another prayer:*
>
> Loving God,
> we thank you for sending Jesus to be our friend.
> Protect us and guide us this day.
> Help us to grow strong in faith and love.
> Give us courage to follow Jesus to the cross
> and receive his gift of life,
> through his death and resurrection. **Amen.**
>
> *Leader:* Let us pray together the prayer Jesus taught us.
>
> *All:* **Our Father, who art in heaven, . . .**

Hymn or Psalm   *(Choose a favorite hymn or psalm to memorize during Lent and repeat it every day.)*

Blessing

> *Leader:* The love of God, the grace of our Lord Jesus Christ, and the communion of the Holy Spirit blesses us now and always.

The peace of Christ be with you.

People: **The peace of Christ be with you.**

Daily Scripture Readings for Lent

Ash Wednesday: Jonah 3:1–4:11 / Luke 18:9-14
Thursday: Heb. 12:1-14 / Mark 2:18-22
Friday: Phil. 1:1-11 / Mark 5:1-20
Saturday: Phil. 2:1-11 / Mark 8:31-38

Weeks of Lent

	Sun	Mon	Tue	Wed	Thur	Fri	Sat
Lent 1:							
Exod.	3:1-15	3:16–4:17	5:1–6:1	7:8-24	9:13-35	10:21–11:8	12:1-20
John	1:35-50	2:1-12	2:13-22	2:23–3:15	3:16-21	3:22-36	4:1-26
Lent 2:							
Heb.	1:1-14	2:11-18	3:1-11	3:12-19	4:1-10	4:11-16	5:1-10
John	4:27-42	4:43-54	5:1-18	5:19-29	5:30-47	6:1-15	6:16-24
Lent 3:							
Deut.	8:1-10	8:11-20	9:6-14	9:15-24	9:25–10:5	10:12-22	11:18-28
John	6:27-40	6: 41-51	6:52-72	7:1-13	7:14-36	7:37-52	8:1-11
Lent 4:							
Rom.	1:1-15	1:16-25	1:28–2:11	2:12-24	2:25–3:18	3:19-31	6:3-14
John	8:12-30	9:1-17	9:18-41	11:1-27	11:28-44	12:1-11	12:20-26
Lent 5:							
Rom.	7:13-25	8:1-11	8:12-27	8:28-39	10:1-17	12:1-21	16:17-27
John	12:27-36	13:1-20	13:21-38	16:16-32	Luke 19:41-48	22:7-23	22:28-46

Holy Week:

Palm Sunday: John 12:12-19
Monday: John 18:1-18
Tuesday: John 18:19-27
Wednesday: John 18:28-38a
Holy Thursday: John 18:38b–19:16a
Good Friday: John 19:16b-42
Holy Saturday: Rom. 8:1-11

Household Prayer for Easter

The following order for household prayer is for use from Easter Day through the Day of Pentecost. It may be copied and distributed, along with the chart of daily Scripture readings for the Fifty Days, for use in parish households. Each day new scripture readings are added to the order, using the chart of daily readings for Easter on pages 152-153. The second reading may also be a meditation chosen from a devotional book. Sing a hymn if at all possible. Otherwise, read a hymn together, choosing one from the index of your hymnal under "Easter."

Prepare a worship center for daily prayer in the household, similar to the one used for Lent but with brighter colors, fresh flowers, and other signs of spring. Cover a small table with a gold or white cloth. Children can help make the cloth by fringing a square of fabric. Choose objects to place on the table that remind you of the season of Easter and invite you to pray together, for example: an open Bible, flowers, a large white candle, a bowl of water and seashells as reminders of baptism. The candle may be the same one used during Lent.

Call to Prayer

> *Leader:* Let us give thanks and remember
> the most important story handed down to us:
> that Christ died for our sins in accordance with the scriptures,
> and that he was buried,
> and that he was raised on the third day
> in accordance with the scriptures.   *(Based on 1 Corinthians 15:3-4)*
> Alleluia! Christ is risen!

> *People:* **Christ is risen indeed! Alleluia!**

Lighting of the Candle

> *Leader:* Again Jesus spoke to them, saying, "I am the light of the world.

Whoever follows me will never walk in darkness
but will have the light of life." *(John 8:12)*

Children of God, Jesus shines on us,
and we will shine like stars in the world. *(Based on Philippians 2:15)*

Hymn Suggestions: "He Lives," "This Little Light of Mine"

Scripture Reading   (from daily readings)

Second Reading
(a second daily Scripture reading, a psalm, or a meditation)

Prayers
Leader: In the beauty of this holy Easter season, let us pray together.

Silent prayers

Spoken prayers: Anyone can speak short prayers of petition and thanksgiving.

The leader prays this or another prayer:

God of life, you raised your Son Jesus from the dead,
   and now he calls us his friends:
Show us the way to live in love and friendship with everyone.
Help us to bring Jesus' gift of peace to the world.
We thank you for the disciples who saw Jesus and ate with him
   and for the gift of the Holy Spirit, our comfort and guide.
In the name of Jesus Christ. **Amen.**

Leader: Let us pray together the prayer Jesus taught us.

All: **Our Father, who art in heaven, . . .**

Hymn or Psalm   (Choose a favorite hymn or psalm to memorize
during Easter and repeat it every day.)
Blessing
Leader: The love of God, the grace of our Lord Jesus Christ, and the communion of the Holy Spirit blesses us now and always.

The peace of Christ be with you.

People: **The peace of Christ be with you.**

Scripture Readings for the Fifty Days of Easter

Easter 1:
Easter Day

Isa. 51:6-11   Col. 3:1-4   Luke 24:13-35

	Mon	Tue	Wed	Thur	Fri	Sat
Acts	1:1-5	3:1-10	4:1-12	6:1-7	6:8-15	7:54-60
John	20:11-18	20:19-23	20:24-30	21:1-14	21:15-19	21:20-24

Easter 2:
Second Sunday

Isa. 43:8-13   1 Pet. 2:2-10   Matt. 28:16-29

	Mon	Tue	Wed	Thur	Fri	Sat
Acts	8:1-8	8:9-25	8:26-40	9:1-9	9:10-22	9:23-31
John	10:1-8	10:11-18	10:19-30	14:1-14	14:15-24	14:25-31

Easter 3:
Third Sunday

Exod. 12:1-14   1 John 2:7-17   Mark 16:9-20

	Mon	Tue	Wed	Thur	Fri	Sat
Acts	9:32-42	10:1-16	10:17-33	10:34-48	11:1-18	11:19-30
John	15:1-11	15:12-27	16:1-15	16:16-33	17:1-19	17:20-25

Easter 4:
Fourth Sunday

Ezek. 34:11-31   1 John 2:18-29   Mark 6:30-44

	Mon	Tue	Wed	Thur	Fri	Sat
Acts	12:1-19	13:1-25	13:26-52	14:1-18	15:1-21	15:22-41
Matt.	5:1-12	5:13-20	5:38-48	6:1-14	6:25-34	7:1-12

Easter 5:
Fifth Sunday   Deut. 6:1-9   Heb. 12:1-14   Luke 4:16-30

	Mon	Tue	Wed	Thur	Fri	Sat
Acts	16:1-15	16:16-40	17:1-21	17:22-34	18:1-17	18:18-28
Matt.	7:15-28	8:5-17	8:18-34	13:1-23	19:13-30	20:1-16

Easter 6:
Sixth Sunday   Deut 26:1-11   2 Tim 1:1-14   Luke 12:22-34

	Mon	Tue	Wed	Thur	Fri	Sat
Acts	19:1-20	19:21-41	20:1-38	21:1-40	22:1-30	23:1-35
Rom.	1:1-17	5:1-11	5:12-21	8:1-17	8:18-39	12:1-21

Easter 7:
Seventh Sunday   Lev. 25:1-17   Eph. 2:1-10   Luke 10:1-9, 17-24

	Mon	Tue	Wed	Thur	Fri	Sat
Acts	24:1-27	25:1-27	26:1-32	27:1-26	27:27-44	28:1-31
Rev.	1:1-8	1:9-20	4:1-11; 5:11-14	7:11-17	21:1-7	22:1-21

The Day of Pentecost   Isa. 11:1-9   1 Cor. 2:1-13   John 14:21-29

An Order for Study Groups and Meetings During Lent

Greeting

Grace to you and peace from our Lord Jesus Christ.

The peace of Christ be with us.

May God turn us toward the cross of Jesus.

Return to the LORD, your God,
for God is gracious and merciful,
slow to anger, and abounding in steadfast love,

Psalm 4 (v. 5 paraphrased by author)

Answer me when I call, O God of my right!
   You gave me room when I was in distress.
   Be gracious to me, and hear my prayer.

How long, you people, shall my honor suffer shame?
   How long will you love vain words, and seek after lies?

But know that the LORD has set apart the faithful to be God's own people;
   the LORD hears when I call.

When you are disturbed, do not sin;
   ponder it on your beds, and be silent.
Offer right sacrifices,
   and put your trust in the LORD.

There are many who say, "O that we might see some good!
   Let the light of your face shine on us, O LORD!"

You have put gladness in my heart
   more than when their grain and wine abound.
I will both lie down and sleep in peace;
   for you alone, O LORD, make me lie down in safety.

Hymn Suggestions: *"Have Thine Own Way, Lord," "Where Cross the Crowded Ways of Life"*

Scripture Reading   ***2 Corinthians 6:1-10***

As we work together with him, we urge you also not to accept
the grace of God in vain.
For he says,
"At an acceptable time I have listened to you,
and on a day of salvation I have helped you."
    See, now is the acceptable time; see, now is the day of salva-
tion! We are putting no obstacle in anyone's way, so that no
fault may be found with our ministry, but as servants of God
we have commended ourselves in every way: through great
endurance, in afflictions, hardships, calamities, beatings,
imprisonments, riots, labors, sleepless nights, hunger; by purity,
knowledge, patience, kindness, holiness of spirit, genuine love,
truthful speech, and the power of God; with the weapons of
righteousness for the right hand and for the left; in honor and
dishonor, in ill repute and good repute. We are treated as
impostors, and yet are true; as unknown, and yet are well
known; as dying, and see—we are alive; as punished, and yet
not killed; as sorrowful, yet always rejoicing; as poor, yet making many rich; as having nothing, and yet possessing everything.

Prayer

God is near to us and will hear us when we call.
Let us ask God's blessing on our work.
Gracious God,
you have promised to guide us when we are perplexed
and show us the right path:
Prepare us to do your work and bring your goodness to all.
Help us to agree in love to listen with open minds and hearts.
 Give us patience with each other and keep us true to your word.
Comfort those in our community who are sick or in distress.
Especially we pray for *(names of persons).*
Help the suffering people of the world and give us peace.
Especially we pray for *(Names of nations).*
Grant us grace to live lives that are pleasing to you
and find hope in the death and resurrection of your Son Jesus
Christ,

in whose name we pray. **Amen.**
Let us pray the prayer that Jesus taught us.

Our Father, who art in heaven, . . .

Charge and Blessing

Fill us with your Spirit of life, O God,
and give us courage to be your disciples
that we may do what is good and right and true,
in the name of Jesus your son, who died for us. **Amen.**

**Let justice roll down like waters,
and righteousness like an ever-flowing stream.**

Additional Scripture Readings
and Psalms for Lent

Psalm 25:1-10   1 Peter 3:18-25

Psalm 27   Philippians 3:17–4:1

Psalm 91   Romans 4:13-25

Psalm 63:1-8   1 Corinthians 1:18-25

Psalm 130   Romans 8:6-11

Psalm 35   Ephesians 5:8-14

* * * *

An Order for Study Groups and Meetings
During Easter

Greeting

We proclaim what was handed down to us:
that Jesus died and was buried,

that on the third day God raised him from the dead
and brought him to sit at God's right hand.
We abide in the love of Jesus,
and we live in his promise of life in abundance, now and forever.

Thanks be to God.

Psalm 22:25-31 (*Author's paraphrase*)

From you comes my praise in the great congregation;
my vows I will pay before those who fear the LORD.

The poor shall eat and be satisfied;
those who seek God shall praise the LORD.
May your hearts live forever!

All the ends of the earth shall remember
and turn to the LORD;
and all the families of the nations
shall worship before our God.
For dominion belongs to the LORD,
who rules over the nations.

To God, indeed, shall all who sleep in the earth bow down;
before God shall bow all who go down to the dust,
and I shall live for the LORD.

Posterity will serve him;
future generations will be told about the Lord.

We will proclaim God's deliverance to a people yet unborn,
saying that the LORD has done it.

Hymn Suggestions: *"O For a Thousand Tongues to Sing,"*
"Come, Ye Faithful, Raise the Strain"

Scripture Reading   *John 15:1-11*

I am the true vine, and my Father is the vinegrower. He removes every branch in me that bears no fruit. Every branch that bears fruit he prunes to make it bear more fruit. You have already been cleansed by the word that I have spoken to you. Abide in me as I abide in you. Just as the branch cannot bear fruit by itself unless it abides in the vine, neither can you unless you abide in me. I am the vine, you are the branches. Those who abide in me and I in them bear much fruit, because apart from me you can do nothing. Whoever does not abide in me is thrown away like a branch and withers; such branches are gathered, thrown into the fire, and burned. If you abide in me, and my words abide in you, ask for whatever you wish, and it will be done for you. My Father is glorified by this, that you bear much fruit and become my disciples. As the Father has loved me, so I have loved you; abide in my love. If you keep my commandments, you will abide in my love, just as I have kept my Father's commandments and abide in his love. I have said these things to you so that my joy may be in you, and that your joy may be complete.

Prayer

The disciples who gathered in an upper room on the day of resurrection were blessed with Jesus' presence and the gift of the Spirit.
Let us pray for God's blessing on this gathering.

God of life,
you have made us your people through your Son Jesus Christ
and made us citizens of your reign:
Prepare us to do the work of Jesus on earth,
and give us courage to bring his justice and love to all.
Make us one in Christ Jesus
that others may know him by our love.
Give us patience and kindness toward each other
that we may work for the common good.
Comfort those in our community who are sick or in distress.
Especially we pray for *(Names of persons)*.
Help the suffering people of the world and give us peace.
Especially we pray for *(Names of nations)*.
We give you thanks for the new life you give us
through the death and resurrection of your Son Jesus Christ,
in whose name we pray. **Amen.**

Let us pray the prayer that Jesus taught us.

Our Father, who art in heaven, . . .

Charge and Blessing

God our good gardener will care for us and strengthen us by the abiding love of Christ Jesus our Lord. May God teach us to be Jesus' disciples and make us faithful branches, growing together and bearing fruit to God's glory.
God's name be praised. Alleluia!

Bless the name of our risen Lord. Alleluia!

Additional Scripture Readings and Psalms for Easter

Psalm 133   John 17:20-26

Psalm 67   1 John 1:1–2:2

Psalm 147:1-11   1 John 3:16-27

Psalm 98   1 John 5:1-6

Psalm 47   Ephesians 1:15-23

Psalm 104:24-34   1 Corinthians 12:3*b*-13